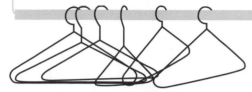

THE
FOREVER
WARDROBE

Find your style.
Transform your clothes.
Save time + money.

ANNA CASCARINA

Illustrations by Ludivine Josephine

THE FOREVER WARDROBE

Find your style.
Transform your clothes.
Save time + money.

BLOOMSBURY PUBLISHING
LONDON · OXFORD · NEW YORK · NEW DELHI · SYDNEY

INTRODUCTION

Imagine waking up every morning, confident that whatever you wear will help you look and feel amazing. No more overwhelming piles of unworn clothes, and the feeling of having 'nothing to wear' is a thing of the past. A capsule wardrobe can make this happen, and I'm going to show you how.

The idea of a capsule wardrobe has gained popularity in recent years – and for good reason. It's about being sustainable, reducing waste and ensuring that your wardrobe serves you well, rather than causing stress and clutter. Together, in this book, we'll create a collection of items that align with your own style, have longevity and make you feel your best.

This book is for everyone, no matter what stage of life you're at. It's here to guide you in curating a capsule wardrobe that brings you joy and is filled with pieces you'll love wearing again and again, and are uniquely tailored to your personal style. You'll know exactly what clothes you own, why you own them, and why they look good on you.

With questionnaires, tips, tricks and knowhow based on more than 25 years of experience in the fashion industry, I'll show you how to find your style so that you can create a wardrobe full of pieces that showcase your individuality, regardless of your budget. I understand the transformative power of a great outfit. It's not just about looking good; it's about expressing yourself and showing the world who you truly are.

Sustainability is another crucial aspect we'll focus on. By investing in high-quality, timeless pieces, we can reduce our impact on the environment and shop more mindfully. This approach will not only benefit our planet, but also save you time, money and energy in the long run.

To help make your wardrobe edit as fun and easy as possible, you'll find worksheets throughout the book to help keep you on track. At the beginning of each worksheet there is a question on how you are feeling about your wardrobe that day – from overwhelmed to on top of it. Circle one of the lines to gauge how you are feeling, and, as you read through the book, get closer to making your wardrobe truly yours.

01

THE PRINCIPLES OF STYLE

Humans are diverse creatures, each with a unique set of wants, needs and experiences. Our individuality is shaped by myriad factors, including the environments we've grown up in, the bodies we inhabit and the circumstances we find ourselves in. It should come as no surprise, then, that our personal styles vary greatly.

When it comes to personal style, we often find ourselves drawn to certain aesthetics or fashion trends that resonate with us. Some people may prefer a minimalist approach, while others lean towards more maximalist expression. But even within these broader categories, subtle nuances and individual preferences shine through, giving each person their own distinctive style.

Seeking inspiration from others, or being swayed by a celebrity's style on social media is always tempting, but it can be challenging to translate someone else's style into our own. We may admire a particular look on someone and try to replicate it, only to find that it doesn't work for us. That's because the other person's style is unique to them; we need instead to discover and embrace our own individual style. Once we have that nailed down, shopping and getting dressed become much easier to navigate. This is where the concept of a capsule wardrobe comes in to play.

A capsule wardrobe is built on the idea of carefully selecting pieces that resonate with our personal style and have versatility and longevity. The goal is to invest in items that can be worn repeatedly, maximising their value and minimising the temptation to buy more clothes than we need.

By taking the time to understand our own tastes and preferences, and how we want to express ourselves through our style, we can curate a wardrobe that is not only functional, but also tells a story of who we are. Building a wardrobe like this requires careful consideration and intention, but it is truly worth it. We learn to discern between fleeting fads and timeless pieces; we invest in quality items that bring us joy and withstand the test of time; we focus on selecting garments that truly speak to us and give us a sense of confidence when we wear them.

TAKEAWAYS

— Our individuality is shaped by many factors.

— There are subtle nuances that determine our distinctive style.

— We need to discover and embrace our own style so that getting dressed each day is easier.

— Our wardrobe should tell the story of who we are.

CHAPTER 1 WORKSHEET

How are you feeling about your wardrobe today?

Overwhelmed   On top of it

How do you want to feel about your personal style by the end of this book?

_____

_____

_____

_____

_____

What do you want your Forever Wardrobe to look like and how you do want to feel?

_____

_____

_____

_____

_____

WHAT IS

A

02

W

CAPSULE
ARDROBE

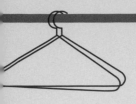

CAPSULE WARDROBE (NOUN): A STREAMLINED COLLECTION OF GARMENTS THAT ARE INTERCHANGEABLE TO CREATE MULTIPLE OUTFIT OPTIONS.

The term 'capsule wardrobe' is not a one-size-fits-all concept; it can mean a completely different thing from one person to the next. Some people might like a neutral palette with a minimalist feel, while others prefer a bolder look with lots of colour and print. Others might like a preppy feel, or some might like a mixture of influences.

Whatever your style, your capsule wardrobe is your own, and different from everyone else's. It can be tweaked for each seasons, too. You may love wearing darker colours with a more structured feel in the winter, but in the summer lean towards a bohemian style with more print and floaty fabrics. Capsule wardrobes can be fluid and ever-changing; some pieces will work across the seasons to help glue everything together, while others will be packed away during the winter or summer months to make way for the new season.

A capsule wardrobe is a reflection of your individuality, a curated edit of clothing which combines to give you new-found confidence, and makes you feel empowered, sexy, strong and comfortable. Whether it's full of neutrals or colour, one thing all capsule wardrobes have in common is that they contain versatile pieces that can be mixed and matched in multiple ways to enhance your style and offer fresh looks.

Embracing a capsule wardrobe not only simplifies your daily dressing routine, but also encourages a more mindful and deliberate approach to fashion. By curating a collection of timeless, high-quality garments, you can avoid short-lived trends and create a genuine connection with your personal style. This reduces the urge to shop impulsively, and minimises the environmental impact of the fast-paced fashion industry.

Why create a capsule wardrobe?

Creating a capsule wardrobe can revolutionise your daily dressing routine by providing multiple outfit options that help you start the day efficiently and stress-free. Whether it's a scorching heat wave or a chilly winter's day, your thoughtfully assembled capsule wardrobe will have you covered, ensuring you always look your best, without the hassle of sifting through a cluttered closet or succumbing to the pressures of last-minute fashion decisions.

Think about how many items of clothing you've bought during the last year. Do you think you bought too much? Or too little? Did you overbuy, only to shove the items in the back of your wardrobe because you weren't sure how to wear them? Or did you avoid buying anything because you feel overwhelmed by the options and unsure what suits you?

Every season we get bombarded with new collections full of trends and 'must-have' pieces that encourage a never-ending buying cycle, which isn't sustainable. Many of us are taking steps to adopt a more environmentally friendly approach to what we buy. By reading this book, you are taking the first step towards a more considered wardrobe with a curated edit of pieces.

In recent years, clothing manufacturing has reached record numbers. Billions of items of clothing are made each day, many of which don't get sold and just end up in landfill. The water consumption of denim production alone is devastating to the planet, and the fast fashion (cheap clothing made rapidly for the mass market, is growing at an alarming rate and contributing to carbon emissions). In the last 20 years, clothing sales doubled from 100 to 200 billion units a year, while the average number of times an item was worn decreased by 36% overall, according to Earth.org. Something has to change: building a wardrobe made up of fewer clothes, but of clothes that have longevity, is better for our precious planet as well as our bank balance.

The foundations of a capsule wardrobe

Now we know the why, it's time to think about the what: what should you include in your capsule wardrobe?

Ideally you're aiming to have about 50–60 items, including shoes and bags. Some of these will work all year round, while others will be season-specific.

Step one — The five items

Grab a rail (or make space on your bed) and pull out your five most-worn items that you go to again and again. These are the pieces that you rely on and feel great in – they're also the building blocks of your capsule wardrobe. They might comprise a satin skirt, black trousers, an oversized jumper, straight jeans and a blazer; or they could be a midi dress, a Breton-stripe top, chino trousers, a trench coat and Converse trainers. Write them down in the worksheet on page 24.

Take a closer look at these pieces, because they provide valuable insight into what truly brings you comfort and joy, and use them to help decipher your unique style. If you find yourself reaching for jeans and a blazer most often, your signature style is probably clean, modern and slightly androgynous. If you tend to gravitate towards flowy dresses, it suggests a preference for a relaxed, feminine look. You feel most at ease in garments that offer freedom and don't feel too structured or restricting. Looking at the pieces you love and wear frequently is a fantastic way to refine your style.

Step two — The building blocks

Once you've settled on your five items, you can start building from there. You need to make sure that your wardrobe can be mixed and matched and gives you lots of options, even if it's full of print. A really good set of basics in a few neutral colours is going to be useful for this, whether your overall style is really colourful or completely monotone.

'Basics' means essential items such as T-shirts, vests, jackets, jeans, trousers or a simple shirt, which play a vital role in completing your outfit. While they may not be the most exciting pieces, they act as the foundation for you to build on. Think of them as the glue that binds your wardrobe together. When combined with a printed skirt or a statement top, these basics will underpin the overall look, enabling versatility and completing your ensemble with style.

Day dress x 2	Evening dress x 2	Day trousers x 2 For summer include linen shorts x 1	Smart/evening trousers x 2	Jeans neutral/white x 1 blue x 2 black x 1
Leggings/ joggers x 2	Day skirt x 2	Evening skirt x 1	Blazers/jackets grey/black/ neutral x 2 evening x 1	Shirts neutral/white x 1 linen x 1 black/dark x 1 printed x 1
Jumpers everyday x 2	Jumpers cashmere/light knit x 2	Jumpers printed/fleece x 1	Sweatshirts x 2	Cardigans chunky knit x 1 fine knit x 1
T-shirts fitted x 2 loose fit x 2	Vests x 3	Evening tops x 2	Coats smart x 1 everyday x 1 trench/ spring x 1 puffer/ waterproof x 1	Boots flat ankle x 1 heeled knee length x 1 heeled ankle x 1
Shoes loafers/flats x 2 summer sandals x 2 heels/ evening x 2	Trainers x 2	Everyday cross-body bags x 2	Evening bags x 2	Tote bag x 1

Step three — Your 50–60-piece capsule wardrobe

The grid on the left is an example breakdown of the items you might have in a capsule wardrobe. These will change as you discover more about your personal style, which we will delve into in the next chapter.

The 80/20 rule

To ensure that your unique personality shines through in your style, I encourage you to embrace the 80/20 rule. This tried-and-true styling theory states that approximately 80% of your wardrobe should consist of timeless pieces, while the remaining 20% can be trend-driven.

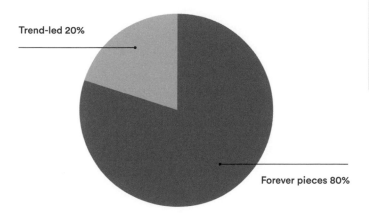

Trend-led 20%

Forever pieces 80%

Let's focus on the 80% first. These are the cherished pieces that you return to year after year. As they are the foundation of your wardrobe, they deserve careful investment. When selecting these items, prioritise longevity in terms of shape, style, fabrication and construction so they can effortlessly blend with changing trends and fashion cycles.

The 20% allows for a touch of spontaneity. These are the trend items or unique pieces that bring you immense joy. They may deviate from your usual style, and that's perfectly fine. There may not always be a clear explanation for their appeal; they might evoke fond memories, feature an eye-catching print or simply be incredibly fun to wear on special occasions. Even though these pieces may not align with the rest of your capsule wardrobe, they should still have a place in your style edit.

By striking a balance between these timeless pieces and trend-led items, you create a wardrobe that reflects your personal style but is versatile and adaptable. This approach allows you to curate a collection that effortlessly merges classic elements with moments of self-expression and creativity. It is of utmost importance to ensure that your sense of self remains front and centre in your capsule wardrobe.

For example, my dominant style is definitely minimal and contemporary. But as a child of the 1970s, I have a deep love of retro style. I may not wear a floaty dress, but I do own three fringed suede jackets, and although I don't wear them regularly, I feel immense pleasure when I do. These jackets have a permanent place in my wardrobe because they bring me joy, and I believe there are perfect occasions, particularly during the summertime, to flaunt them.

When deciding what to include in your capsule wardrobe, the 80/20 rule will help to keep you grounded in the ever-changing landscape of fashion. It serves as a gentle reminder to stay focused on what truly resonates with your personal style, even when you're tempted by new and exciting pieces that hit the stores.

TAKEAWAYS

— A capsule wardrobe is a curated edit of clothing that you love and reach for over and over again.

— Capsule wardrobes are for everyone, whatever your style.

— A capsule wardrobe will simplify your routine, save you time and money, help you to foster a more mindful approach to fashion, and make you feel good.

— A good set of basics will provide you with the building blocks of an outfit.

— You should include about 50–60 items, including shoes and bags in your capsule wardrobe.

— Follow the 80/20 rule: aim for 80% timeless pieces and 20% trend led.

CHAPTER 2 WORKSHEET

How are you feeling about your wardrobe today?

Overwhelmed   On top of it

| | | | | | | | | |

What items of clothing did you buy over the last year?

_____

_____

_____

_____

_____

How many times have you worn them?

_____

_____

_____

_____

_____

What are the five items that you wear repeatedly?

_____

_____

_____

_____

_____

Why do you wear them a lot?

_____

_____

_____

_____

_____

Wardrobe inventory

Using the grid on page 20 as a guide, write down what you currently have in your wardrobe.

Think about the most worn pieces in your wardrobe and work out which items are part of your 80% and which are in the other 20%.

_____   _____

_____   _____

_____   _____

_____   _____

_____   _____

FI

YOUR

STY

NDING

LE 03

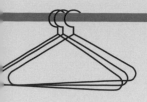

Do you know what your own style is? Are you confident about who you are when it comes to fashion? Do you stick to one aesthetic, or are you more of a chamaeleon who likes to mix it up a bit? The two sections in this chapter will help you discover your style, so that you have the confidence to create a capsule wardrobe that's true to you and contains multiple outfits you feel comfortable in.

Everyone has their own personal style, and this can evolve over time. Sometimes, though, we can lose our way and find it difficult to pinpoint exactly what style we want to achieve, and how to achieve it. To solve this, first this chapter shows you how to create your own Fashion Manifesto, and then helps you hone in on your style inspiration.

People have diverse approaches to their personal style. Some people prefer to stick to a specific style that resonates with them, while others enjoy blending different styles based on their mood. Neither approach is wrong; it's all about how you choose to express and play around with your style.

Fashion is a source of fun and excitement that allows you to explore and experiment. There are no strict rules; it's a realm of individualism in which you have the freedom to curate a wardrobe that reflects your personality and preferences. Whether you find joy in maintaining a consistent style or mixing different styles, the key is to stay true to yourself and follow your instincts. Fashion is ultimately about self-expression, so it's important to wear what feels genuine and makes you happy.

You might like wearing simple outfits in beautiful fabrics with little-to-no prints as well as love a feminine look, so you might choose a pair of black trousers with a neutral jumper one day and a pretty floral dress the next. Having a capsule wardrobe doesn't mean you have to stick to one style, but you will have a dominant style that you gravitate towards, and this is what you need to focus on first.

My signature style is definitely minimal, but occasionally I also include some vintage-inspired pieces like T-shirts, retro prints and leather and suede jackets. I also love a relaxed, informal jeans-and-trainer combo; it all depends on my mood that day. When building my Forever Wardrobe, I prioritise my minimal style. Then I incorporate the other styles, either as part of the 20%ers (trend items that may not last longer than a season or two, after which I sell or donate them), or as one of the 80% investment pieces, ensuring they have longevity and blend in effortlessly with the rest of my 80%ers.

People sometimes want a specific look, but have absolutely no idea how to get there. This can be frustrating as well as costly – we can buy countless pieces of clothing without knowing whether they suit us, or even if we like them, with the aim of chasing a style that isn't clear to us in the first place. These items can gather dust in the wardrobe, still with their tags on. Really knowing your style, what you love and what suits you, and building a wardrobe around that, means you'll have many different outfit options that all work for you.

Your Fashion Manifesto

There are several methods that stylists use to help you decipher your style, from summing it up in three adjectives to creating moodboards. My approach is to create a Fashion Manifesto: a short paragraph that uses descriptive words to help hone in on your personal style. Three adjectives can be quite limiting, so by creating a longer statement you can be open to all the nuances of your personal style. Here are some adjectives that might inspire you:

70s	Edgy	Hipster	Sophisticated
90s	Elegant	Modern	Sporty
Androgynous	Ethereal	Monochromatic	Street
Artsy	Flirty	Oversized	Structured
Chic	Folkloric	Playful	Tomboy
Clean	Fun	Preppy	Traditional
Colourful	Futuristic	Punk	Unique
Contemporary	Geeky	Quirky	Urban
Country	Girlie	Relaxed	Utilitarian
Cyberpunk	Glamorous	Retro	Victorian-inspired
Dapper	Gothic	Rocker	Vintage
Eclectic	Grungy	Romantic	Whimsical

Step One — The five key items

Turn to the list of five key items you pulled out earlier (see page 19). Think of two words that describe these items: are they relaxed, minimal, tailored, oversized, casual, structured, monotone, retro, floaty? Use the list opposite for inspiration. These two words can be completely different – so if your five items were primarily jeans and boho tops, your words might be relaxed and floaty. Or if you pulled out mainly bright dresses and funky accessories, your words could be colourful and unique. Note them down in the worksheet on page 41.

Step Two — Extras

Now think about other pieces in your wardrobe that don't seem to fit with your main style, but that you love nonetheless. Perhaps your wardrobe is mainly minimal, but you have a few vintage T-shirts in there, or you have a very casual wardrobe and a penchant for high-end designer bags. Find two different words to describe those pieces.

If you don't veer off from your aesthetic much, that's absolutely fine. Just think of two additional words to describe it. Try to think of words that delve deeper into what your style says about you, such as quirky or sporty, and note these down on the worksheet on page 41.

Step Three — Mood

Now think of two words that describe what you want your outfits to say about you. We'll call this your style mood. Do you try to be edgy, creative, sleek, modern, pretty, alternative, sexy, polished or understated? Or perhaps you want your outfit to suggest that you are futuristic, bold, mystical or street? Note these two words down on the worksheet on page 41.

While doing these three steps, try to be as truthful as possible and really think about how these words describe you. If your words feel too generic, break them down further to be more descriptive; you want to be as specific as possible.

Step Four — Create your manifesto

Now you have your six words, use this template to state your Fashion Manifesto.

_____ and _____ with a touch of _____ to give a _____ feel that is _____ and _____ .

For example, my six words are:

— **Relaxed** — In my wardrobe I have a lot of oversized shapes, loose jeans and T-shirts.
— **Minimal** — I love neutral colours, clean lines and understated pieces.
— **1970s California** — This describes my vintage T-shirts and suede-fringed jackets.
— **Contemporary** — There are some modern touches, such as cut-out details.
— **Elevated** — My wardrobe consists of sophisticated, grown-up pieces like blazers, satin skirts, kitten heels and gold jewellery.
— **Effortless** — I try to create a simple style, with longevity and classic pieces.

Therefore, my Fashion Manifesto is:

Relaxed and **minimal** with a touch of **70s California** to give a **contemporary** feel that is **elevated** and **effortless**.

I wear a lot of blazers, jeans, T-shirts, dresses and shirts: a simple, relaxed style, but always with a modern element. My blazer might be a classic black style, but with an oversized shape; my jeans might be ultra baggy, but have a contemporary twist like a high waist or added detaillng; my vest might be a classic rib, but with a one-shoulder double strap for a contemporary look; I might add a vintage T-shirt or fringed jacket for that 70s California vibe, or stick to a minimal style with simple clean silhouettes.

All these elements come together to describe my style. I don't always wear vintage T-shirts or a fringed jacket, but my manifesto reminds me they're there, part of who I am and what I love.

Now it's your turn! Start working on your Fashion Manifesto (there's space at the end of the chapter for this). If you get stuck, the next section (Your Style Inspiration) and the Style Questionnaire in the worksheet at the end of the chapter will help. Follow the prompts to gather as much information as possible about what kind of style you love, then return to your manifesto.

Your style inspiration

In this section you will delve into what your unique style personality is, so you can begin to curate a wardrobe that is truly aligned with your individuality.

Read through the following questions and note down your responses on the worksheet at the end of the chapter (see page 42).

Keep in mind that the designer names mentioned throughout this chapter are just to give you an idea of the kind of style you might gravitate towards. You can find similar styles on the high street – I'm definitely not suggesting you all start shopping in Chanel or Dior! (Although wouldn't that be the dream?)

1. Think about your style icons, whether past or present. Do you love the classic style of Audrey Hepburn, or a bohemian style like Jane Birkin's? Do you love a rock-chick vibe like Kate Moss or a preppy style like Alexa Chung? Are you influenced by the androgynous style of Zoë Kravitz or the contemporary style of Solange Knowles?

2. Now think about the why. Why do you love their style? What is it that attracts you to them? Google individual images of the people whose style you love and save them to a Pinterest board. Study the pictures and think about what draws you in.

3. Let's move on to designers. Thinking about high-end designers, who do you admire and whose designs do you love? Do you love a structured, avant-garde look like Alexander McQueen, or a minimalist look like The Row? Do you love over-the-top bold styles like Gucci's, or a bohemian vibe like Isabel Marant?

4. Now, again, the why. What is it that draws you to those designers? Really unpick what you love about them. Is it the sharp tailoring, beautiful prints, floaty fabrics or simple lines? Is it the clothing in particular that you gravitate towards, or the vision and aesthetic around the brand?

5. Let's move on to your own wardrobe. Recall your five key items. What is it about them that you love? Is it familiarity? Is it comfort? Do they make you feel sexy? Or confident? Do you wear them because you love how you feel in them, or because they're easy to wear and you don't have anything else?

   Analyse why you feel like that. Is it the cut, colour, style? Does they fit you perfectly? Are they an investment piece? Are they something that evokes memories? Write down any feelings that come to mind when you wear these items.

6. Think about any pieces in your wardrobe that you don't wear, or items you've bought that have remained unworn? Why do you think that is? Is it because the fit isn't quite right? Does the colour not suit you? Do you feel uncomfortable wearing them? Try those pieces on again and really study yourself in them. Write down how they make you feel, and why you think you don't wear them.

7. Take a close look at the clothes that you wear often and those that don't see much daylight, and examine their style disparities. What sets apart the pieces you love from those you don't wear? As you delve into this, consider your lifestyle as well. If you have a penchant for high heels but spend your days chasing after energetic children, it's unlikely that heels will feature in your everyday clothing choices. Similarly, if you're fond of sophisticated tailoring but mostly work from home and seldom need to don a tailored suit, it may not be practical to invest in such pieces. Considering all these factors, can you identify the misjudgements you've made when purchasing the garments that end up neglected in your wardrobe? Write them down.

When you pinpoint those errors, repeating them becomes easier to avoid next time you shop. It may be that you love a big puff-sleeve taffeta dress, but it doesn't suit your shape. Or you may want to wear an all-beige outfit, but the colour completely washes you out. Or you've got a love for silk dresses, but you also have a toddler with greasy fingers! Understanding and embracing your personal style is crucial. While we may be drawn to a certain style and aesthetic, we need to recognise that it might not complement our individuality or suit our lifestyle. This is where the art of compromise comes in.

Here are two examples:

A — You gravitate towards a neutral palette of creams, beiges, whites and blacks. You love a minimalist look with a streamlined silhouette and a simple aesthetic. However, you

35

actually suit bold colours and print more than neutrals. Instead of dismissing the entire style, there's room for adaptation.

— If wearing beige near your face washes you out, consider opting for navy on the upper half with beige trousers or skirt.
— Embrace simple prints with no more than two colours, ensuring that the overall silhouette remains clean.
— Stick to luxurious fabrics and a slightly androgynous shape while injecting colour through single-colour tops or accessorising with a vibrant accent. Remember not to exceed two colours at once.
— Maintain a harmonious tonal balance to create a streamlined, minimal look.

B — You have an affinity for boldness, embracing elements like oversized collars, vibrant clashes of prints, voluminous dresses and abundant colour. However, despite admiring this style on others, you feel self-conscious and unsure whether you can pull it off successfully. There's a nagging sense that something doesn't quite click. To address this, why not try a balanced approach? Keep your foundation simple and understated and incorporate statement pieces that capture your bold aesthetic.

By combining simple basics with standout items, you can strike a harmonious balance that allows you confidently to showcase your personal style without feeling overwhelmed or out of place.

— Combine a great pair of jeans with a shirt featuring a striking oversized collar.
— Pair a stunning, brightly printed full skirt with a crisp white T-shirt.

8. Let's look at social media. Who do you follow, and whose style do you love? Do you gravitate towards a minimal aesthetic, or do you get inspired by people that are experimental and bold in their style? Or perhaps you

follow a bit of both? Think about how these accounts make you feel. Are they seductive, repetitive, consistent? What whets your appetite to keep following? Write down a few of your social media favourites and then ask yourself why you love their style.

9. Do you have any full-length pictures of yourself? If you don't, ask family members or friends to send you any they have. Have a look at these images of you. What do you see looking back at you? What are you wearing, and do you like it? How has your style evolved over the years? Is there a particular style that you love, or really dislike? Taking all the emotion out, try to look at the pictures as if they're of someone else; don't look at the size of your body or how old you look, just look at the person and the clothes. Write down your thoughts.

10. Ask your friends and family what they think about your style. Ask people with different fashion tastes for their honest feedback. Do they think you've changed over the years? Have you become less experimental and brave? Or more so? What outfit have you worn that they loved you in? What style of clothing do they think you look best in? Do you agree?

By taking a step back and dissecting your style evolution over the years, you can really understand the style choices you have made, whether good or bad. Asking family and friends will help you look at the style of clothing you love and work out whether others think it works on you. It will help separate the good outfits from the not-so-good, and give you insight into the shapes and styles that flatter you the most.

Remember, this exercise is about empowerment and being truthful with yourself; it's not about body shaming or embarrassment. Whoever you ask for honesty needs to make sure they are giving their opinion based purely on your fashion style, and what they think makes you shine with confidence.

Balancing your styles

Now that you've gained a better understanding of the style you gravitate towards naturally, and why it appeals to you, let's address an important point. Even though this section has revealed your dominant style, it's also good to consider other styles you like and why.

For example, I have a fondness for vintage style because it brings me a sense of nostalgia, and I feel amazing in my suede-fringed jacket. Even though my primary style leans more towards minimalism, it can be exciting to mix things up by incorporating these unexpected items. This is when your personal style truly shines: the contrast between two different styles can be inspiring.

If you're a complete chamaeleon and have multiple style personalities that you like to mix up regularly, then my advice would be to create a few 'mini' capsule collections within your wardrobe. The same rules apply, though you might have three or four smaller capsule collections consisting of 10–15 pieces that all mix and match together with your basics. This way you can still change up your look regularly while effortlessly creating inspiring outfits whatever style mood you're in that day.

Of course, there's absolutely nothing wrong with sticking to one style exclusively if that's what makes you feel confident and comfortable. However, if you're eager to step out of your safety net and explore new possibilities, experimenting with mixing styles can bring a fresh sense of balance to your outfits. It allows you to infuse your own personality and create looks that truly reflect who you are. We'll delve deeper into the concept of outfit mood and incorporating unexpected items in later chapters.

Bringing it all together

By now you have gained insights into the elements, aesthetics and overall vibe that resonate with you the most. These will serve as the foundations for identifying and defining your style. And with this deeper understanding, it becomes easier to articulate and create your Fashion Manifesto. When you include the unusual elements of your wardrobe that do not fit with your dominant style, you can begin to express yourself through your outfit choices in a more diverse, nuanced and interesting way. This is when your personality will really start to shine through.

Your wardrobe and your lifestyle

Another important aspect of your personal style preferences is your lifestyle. You may love a classic, put-together, chic look with elegant heels and structured little bag, but your lifestyle might not lend itself to that style. As life unfolds and changes occur, our roles and responsibilities also evolve, and our wardrobes must adapt accordingly. However, this doesn't mean those previous-life pieces can't be incorporated occasionally. Your Fashion Manifesto guides you to explore the intricacies of your personal style and cherish the items that define who you are. Nevertheless, the majority of your wardrobe should cater to your present needs. It's essential for your style to reflect these aspects of your life.

For those facing a significant life change that may not be permanent, a practical approach is to start afresh without getting rid of the older items. Instead, consider storing them in airtight containers. Chances are, these pieces will come into use again, and you wouldn't want to part with them permanently. This approach allows you to gently press pause on one phase of your life while you navigate a new one. For example, if you're taking an extended leave from work, temporarily set your high-flying workwear aside. Although you may return to that phase later, for now it's more efficient to free up space in your wardrobe and focus on outfits that cater to your current lifestyle, to avoid any confusion when dressing each day.

On the other hand, if a significant lifestyle change is permanent, it's time to start anew. This entails packing away items from your old life and assembling a wardrobe that truly reflects who you are at this moment. While some items may still fit into your new lifestyle, it's crucial to re-evaluate your wardrobe with fresh eyes, considering your current needs and how each piece serves you best.

Ultimately, your wardrobe should be a reflection of your life now, accommodating the activities and roles that define your daily existence, while still reflecting your personal style.

TAKEAWAYS

— Your style can be rigid or more fluid – there's no right or wrong.

— Fashion is about experimenting and having fun.

— Working out exactly what your personal style is can help you create a more considered and hard-working wardrobe.

— The Fashion Manifesto is a three-step method to help you create a statement to describe your style.

— It's important to consider your lifestyle when defining your style personality.

CHAPTER 3 WORKSHEET

How are you feeling about your wardrobe today?

Overwhelmed   On top of it

| | | | | | | | | | |

Your Fashion Manifesto

Use this space to create your own Fashion Manifesto (see page 31).

Step 1: Staples

_____   _____

Step 2: Extras

_____   _____

Step 3: Mood

_____   _____

Use your six words to create your Fashion Manifesto:

_____ and _____ with a touch of _____

to give a _____ feel that is _____ and _____ .

Your style inspiration

Note down your responses to the questions on pages 34–37 here.

Question 1

_____

Question 2

_____

Question 3

_____

Question 4

_____

Question 5

_____

Question 6

_____

Question 7

_____

Question 8

_____

Question 9

_____

Question 10

_____

Your style questionnaire

This style questionnaire is a confirmation tool to provide you with a clearer understanding of your personal style and ensure that your Fashion Manifesto is in full harmony with your style preferences. This will make it even easier for you to edit your wardrobe and make fashion decisions in the future.

Read the following questions and circle the answer that feels most like you.

If I looked in your wardrobe, what colours would I mostly see?

1. Black, white and navy, with a few primary colours like red and green
2. Beiges, whites, creams, browns, with a bit of black and navy
3. Bright colours and prints
4. Soft colours and pastels, mostly lights with a few dark colours, earthy tones
5. Mostly black and dark colours
6. Khaki, naturals, a mix of prints, a few brights

Which collection of words best describes your style?

1. Traditional, timeless, stylish, sophisticated, classic
2. Tonal, neutral, simple, polished, sleek, clean
3. Experimental, bold, trendy, colourful, eclectic
4. Pretty, girly, boho, floaty, soft
5. Smart, sharp, tailored, striking, strong
6. Casual, relaxed, comfortable, easy

What is your favourite outfit?

1. Simple dress with heels and a classic bag
2. Wide-leg trousers, simple shirt, plain sandals, leather tote bag
3. Statement top, fitted trousers, colourful accessories
4. Maxi dress with big collar and ankle boots
5. Smart tailored suit, white shirt and loafers
6. Khaki trousers, trainers and Breton top

You're on a shopping spree and looking for a new favourite. What do you buy?

1. A pair of court shoes or cashmere knit
2. Some good basics
3. A statement piece
4. A floaty dress or suede-fringed jacket
5. Some tailoring
6. A new pair of trainers or slogan T-shirt

Whose style do you most admire?

1. Victoria Beckham
2. Phoebe Philo
3. Tracee Ellis Ross
4. Kate Moss
5. Diane Keaton
6. Kate Middleton

What is your signature coat (or what would you like it to be)?

1. A cashmere wrap coat
2. A black maxi coat, long and simple
3. A leopard-fur or patchwork jacket
4. A single-breasted floral print coat
5. Something sharp and tailored
6. A leather biker jacket

If you had to wear one designer brand for the rest of your life, which one would it be?

1. Chanel
2. The Row
3. Gucci
4. Isabel Marant
5. Balmain
6. Ralph Lauren

What would be your perfect handbag?

1. A classic Chanel flap
2. A neutral tote by The Row
3. A bright Bottega Veneta bag
4. A suede-fringed Chloé bag
5. A studded Valentino Garavani bag
6. A Coach cross-body bag

What's your wardrobe absolute must-have?

1. Trench coat
2. Blazer
3. Statement bag
4. Floral dress
5. Tailoring
6. Breton top

RESULTS

MOSTLY 1s: CLASSIC

You are classic, stylish and timeless, and love a sophisticated look that is simple but still makes a statement. You may add a pop of colour occasionally, but mainly stick to a few colours. You tend to steer clear of trends and veer towards timeless pieces that have longevity, loving investment pieces that will last for years. Think Chanel, Victoria Beckham, Hermès, Dior.

MOSTLY 2s: MINIMAL

You are a minimalist at heart and have a pared-down wardrobe consisting of really good key basics and simple pieces. You prefer monochrome and neutrals, and you don't heavily invest in print or colour. Your mantra is less is more, with sleek clean lines and minimal accessories, and you're likely to invest in high-quality pieces that are fairly androgynous in style. Think The Row, Jil Sander, Bite Studios, Tove, Khaite.

MOSTLY 3s: BOLD

You exude fashion, and love nothing more than being bold and colourful in your clothing choices. You are fashion-forward and adventurous; you invest in trends and love a statement piece. You believe that fashion is art and a way of life. When you walk into a room, you are going to be noticed in the most fabulous outfit, whether it's from an obscure up-and-coming designer or a vintage designer piece. Think Christopher Kane, Balenciaga, Louis Vuitton, Jacquemus, Prada.

MOSTLY 4s: BOHEMIAN

You love a whimsical look that is casual and carefree. You have a romantic view of fashion, loving floaty dresses, pretty prints and detailing. Your colours could be earthy tones, pastels or lighter colours, with the odd black or navy thrown in. You love flowy styles that are playful, and you experiment with mixing prints and detailing such as organic elements and leather. Think Chloé, Isabel Marant, Zimmerman, Valentino, Sea NY, Ulla Johnson.

MOSTLY 5s: SHARP

You mean business when it comes to fashion, and love nothing more than killer heels and a sharp suit. Tailoring and structured detailing is at the forefront of your style, with creative elements that give you a super-sharp, edgy look. Think Balmain, McQueen, Tom Ford, Maison Margiela, Saint Laurent, Bottega Veneta.

MOSTLY 6s: RELAXED

Your day-to-day uniform is a Breton top, a pair of comfy khaki trousers and your favourite trainers. Maybe you wear the occasional pretty dress, but always with ankle boots or trainers. You are all about comfort, but still want to have fun with fashion; you know what you like and you stick to it. You often invest in independent brands rather than high-end fashion. You add the odd investment piece, perhaps with a bag or some jewellery, but you stick to a relaxed style that's easy and casual. Think JW Anderson, Ralph Lauren, Ganni, Sézane, Margaret Howell.

Bringing it all together

What is your dominant style? Are there hints of another style in there too?
Write a description of your style below.

_____

_____

_____

_____

_____

_____

Look at your Fashion Manifesto and your style-questionnaire answers.
How do they compare?

_____

_____

_____

_____

_____

_____

How does your style fit in with your lifestyle? What changes could you make to allow your style preferences to fit into the lifestyle you have now?

_____

_____

_____

_____

_____

_____

YOUR
WARDROBE

HOW TO ORGANISE

04

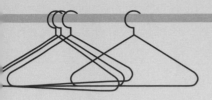

Now that you have a good understanding of your personal style, it's time to organise your wardrobe and select the pieces that perfectly align with that aesthetic. By identifying the items that fit your style, and winnowing out any that don't, you will be able to spot any gaps that need filling. You'll also see that you have things you've bought that don't make you feel good or that you bought on a whim but have never worn because they don't

suit your style.

Think about what drove you to buy those pieces. Are they a style you love but don't know how to wear, or how to make them work with what you already have in your wardrobe? What might you need to make these pieces more wearable?

Of course, you don't want to buy unnecessary things to make one item work. When you're filling a gap in your wardrobe, choose pieces that will become part of your timeless collection, like basic essentials. If you find that you still can't make the outliers work, it's best to sell or donate them. It's not worth holding on to clothes that take up precious space if you won't wear them. You want to create space for the items you genuinely enjoy wearing.

When you're organising your wardrobe, it's a good idea to break it down into different sections. This way, everything is easily accessible and you can build on it with ease. While it would be fantastic to start fresh and empty out your entire wardrobe, that's not feasible for most people, and definitely not sustainable. Taking your wardrobe step by step, section by section, will allow you to create space and tackle the task with a relaxed mindset, minimising stress. We want this to be an enjoyable experience, not a chore!

Get started

Prepare a serene environment by lighting a scented candle, brewing your favourite hot drink and playing some soothing music. Begin your decluttering session in a tidy space, as trying to sort through things in a messy room only adds to the stress. It's important to be relaxed and fully prepared before embarking on this task. You want to be in the right frame of mind because otherwise you might make hasty decisions and accidentally discard items you actually want to keep.

Create four piles for your clothing:

— **Keep**: items that are definitely staying.
— **Sell**: items that are in good condition and you can sell.
— **Donate**: items that are in good condition and you can donate.
— **Maybe**: this is the pile you're not sure about. Keep these somewhere safe for six months. If you haven't thought about them or wanted to wear them during that time, they can be sold or donated.

The hanging space

Start with your clothes rail. I suggest hanging the following items: dresses (unless a heavy knit), shirts and blouses, blazers and jackets, tailored items, trousers, skirts, linen and silk pieces. Jeans take up quite a lot of room, so can be either hung or folded depending on the size of your hanging space.

Hang all the items you're planning to keep on a rail and carefully evaluate each one.

— Does it fit into the aesthetic you discovered in the personal style chapter? Take the time to try it on.
— Does it fit you well?
— Does it truly suit you?
— Do you feel comfortable when wearing it? Remember, just because you love a look, doesn't necessarily mean it will suit you. If you try on anything that doesn't work for you, add it to one of the other piles.

This may be challenging, as it can be really difficult to be ruthless with your wardrobe, especially if you've invested a significant amount of money on it. However, in the long run, it will be more cost effective. The goal is to carefully consider and curate each item, ensuring that you have a great outfit for every day. And this requires a lot of bravery. You need to be really honest with yourself about what it is you want to achieve with your capsule wardrobe.

By doing this, you will make your future buying decisions easier. Repeat buys – when you buy a garment very similar to something already in your wardrobe – are common, because we know what we feel safe in and we're happy with how we look in them. These are the comfort-blanket items that give us that warm feeling of familiarity. If you're a classic minimalist, you may have eight blazers in your closet. Do you really need every single one? Or you may love floaty dresses and can't help but buy them over and over again. Consider selling a few, and instead invest in a couple of really beautiful dresses you love from your favourite designer. By evaluating and reducing the number of repeated items, you'll streamline your wardrobe and make space for the truly beautiful and cherished pieces.

Things to consider:

— Do you have two or more similar items that you can condense down to one?
— Are there six pairs of blue jeans that are all very similar, and you only really wear two of them?
— Do you have four red midi dresses that all look the same?
— Can you be honest with yourself and say goodbye to some of these repeat buys that you don't really need?

Shelves and drawers

Once you've completed your hanging section, move on to the shelves or drawers, taking it one section at a time. How you choose to store your items is entirely up to you, but I recommend grouping similar things together. For example, you can gather all your T-shirts and vests in one section, and your jumpers and sweatshirts in another.

In my wardrobe, I have the following sections:

Short-sleeved T-shirts Long-sleeved T-shirts Vests	Polo necks Light jumpers Cashmere sweaters	Bulky jumpers Sweatshirts	Evening tops Nightwear Workout wear	Accessories: Bags Shoes Scarves Belts

Try not to cram too much into your space. You want to be able to see as many of your clothes as possible so that things don't get lost and forgotten about. Remember the age-old saying 'out of sight, out of mind': if you can't see it, you probably won't wear it, so storing as much as you can in an organised and space-saving way will open up more outfit options as well as creating a tidy space.

TOP TIPS FOR FOLDING

I highly recommend storing jumpers and sweaters folded as opposed to hanging them, as the shoulders of anything weighty can stretch out when hung, as well as taking up valuable hanging space. If you don't have much shelving, hanging shelves can be a really good option. This can work for jeans too, as they can often take up a lot of room.

There are many different folding and storing methods out there, from the KonMari method founded by Marie Kondo to the rolling method; it's totally up to you how you do it. The main thing is to make sure each item is visible and easily accessible without the whole pile getting messed up every time you take something out to wear. Make sure you have at least a couple of centimetres or so above the top of your knits when storing them in drawers, so that they don't pull on the bottom of the drawer above.

Chest of drawers

Do you have a chest of drawers that is stuffed to the brim and lacking order? Get everything out, and after deciding what to sell/donate, arrange what remains into vests, short sleeve T-shirts, long-sleeved T-shirts, going-out tops and so on.

Once you have your piles of clothing, consider laying them side by side to make it easier to see each item. This method really works for slightly bulkier items like jeans and jumpers. It means you can locate the item easily and remove it from the drawer without creating a mess. For smaller items like vest tops and T-shirts, garment boxes work well, as you can get the whole box out to find the item you want. Put them on shelves, drawers or even under the bed. This is a great tip for seasonal items too, as you can just swap your boxes in and out when needed. Don't use plastic boxes, though, as plastic can trap humidity, which won't prolong the life of your clothes. Another option is to use drawer dividers that provide some structure so your items are a bit more contained.

TAKEAWAYS

— Set the scene; create a serene space with a nice cuppa in which to begin.

— Don't hold on to clothes you don't wear, or that don't work with the personal style you've identified. Either sell or donate them.

— Break your wardrobe down into sections and take it step by step.

— If you have repeat buys, condense them down to only one or two pieces of similar items.

— If you can, get a hanging rail and use that to put your items on. It's easier to see what you've got.

— Fold jumpers rather than hanging them.

— Divide your shelving and drawers into sections for T-shirts, vests, jumpers and so on.

CHAPTER 4 WORKSHEET

How are you feeling about your wardrobe today?

Overwhelmed   On top of it

Notes for your clear-out

De-cluttering tools

- ☐ Nice, calm environment
- ☐ Tidy space
- ☐ Light a scented candle
- ☐ Play your favourite tunes
- ☐ Grab a cuppa

Must-have checklist

- ☐ Good hangers, such as slim velvet ones
- ☐ Natural moth repellents
- ☐ Drawer dividers/boxes
- ☐ Cashmere/knitwear storage bags
- ☐ Hanging garment bags

Items to keep	Items to donate	Items to sell

Clothes rail

List the items you'll be hanging on rails.

_____

_____

_____

_____

Shelves and drawers

Divide your clothes into categories and write down what you will put
together on each shelf or drawer.

BASI

05

CS

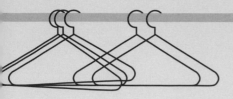

Your wardrobe staples are anything but basic: they are the building blocks of every outfit. These are the pieces that glue everything together from underneath, working outwards. They are important in your wardrobe because you can wear them repeatedly, they go with everything and they give you a starting point each time you get dressed.

Basics are similar for everybody, but if you are a colour-lover they might include a bit more colour than other people's. For example, a really good basic is the classic vest. I would include in my basics a white, grey and black vest. If you love colour, your basic vests might be white, green and pink. It's definitely worth remembering, though, that even if you love colour and print, you should have some neutral basics to help tie everything together. A white vest or T-shirt, for example, looks incredible with a bright pair of statement-print trousers, a full, emerald-green skirt or a pair of yellow linen trousers.

When you talk about basics most people think of vests, T-shirts, underwear and so on. But basics can also include the following pieces, which will give you a foundation to build from in your wardrobe. These items are seasonless and will see you through the whole year.

Underwear (get fitted regularly to ensure you're wearing the correct size)	T-shirts white x 1 grey x 1 black x 1 (or white plus two other colours you wear a lot)	Vests white x 1 grey x 1 black x 1 (or white plus two other colours you wear a lot)	Body/long-sleeve fitted top Black, white or a colour of your choice	Shirt White or a colour of your choice	Classic jeans blue x 1 black x 1
Block colour day dress Black or a colour of your choice	Slinky evening dress Black, white or a block colour	Midi/maxi skirt	Wide-leg trousers	Slim-leg trousers	Blazer Black or neutral tone, or a colour of your choice if you're a colour-lover
Trench coat	Leather jacket	Trainers, a neutral style	Flat shoes such as ballet pumps or loafers	Fine-knit cardigan	Sweatshirt
Crew-neck sweater	Evening shoes	Evening bag	Cross-body bag	Tote bag	Classic, simple belt

The audit

When going through your basics, look at anything that needs updating and consider whether it can be mended or repaired.

— **Stains**: can it be dry cleaned to remove the stain before throwing out?
— **Underwear**: do you need to be re-measured and update your bras and knickers?
— **T-shirts/bodies/shirts/vests**: look for discolouration or anything losing its shape – do they need replacing?
— **Jeans**: do they fit perfectly, and does the style and shape suit you?
— **Dress/skirt**: are there any stains? Is it a classic shape that will last?
— **Trousers**: think about longevity; is the style and shape right? Do you need to update?

— **Blazer**: do you own one? If not, would it be a useful addition to your wardrobe?
— **Coats/jackets**: think about classic styles that will last. Do you need an updated version?
— **Shoes**: what style of shoes will last and go with everything? Stick to the 80% rule here.
— **Knitwear/sweats**: is there any pilling or damage such as moth holes? Do they need updating or can you invest in a de-fuzzer and spend an afternoon de-bobbling?
— **Bags**: again, think of classic items that have longevity. Do you need/want to invest?

With your list of basics in mind, identify what might be missing or need replacing. Make a list of what you need in the notes section at the end of the chapter; this will help when you next go shopping. If you have a list, you are less likely to veer off course and you'll stay focused on what you actually need. This is how you'll keep your wardrobe streamlined and working hard for you, so you can continue to create incredible outfits every day.

The right mix

Your basics will play a big role in your 50–60-item capsule wardrobe (see page 20). You might have a couple of comfy cotton shirts, or a cool oversized denim shirt that you love, and which is a fantastic addition to your wardrobe. A pair of black, wide-leg trousers might be among your foundational basics, while a vibrant green pair, although not classified as a basic, also has a prominent place in your capsule wardrobe.

You can build a really strong outfit from all your basic items together, but you can also mix in some of your 20% trend-led pieces, such as a leopard-print shirt, a metallic cowboy boot or, if you're a colour lover, a really bright furry coat. Remember, your 20%ers are the items that spark joy and reveal a bit more of your style personality. They might be items you may sell on after a few months and that you don't invest heavily in, but that bring your wardrobe up to date during the seasons.

STYLE MATHEMATICS

Let's try out some formulas using basics from the list on page 64:

BASE OUTFIT

White shirt
+
wide-leg trousers
+
blazer
+
ballet pumps
+
tote bag
=
<u>great work outfit</u>

Long-sleeve body
+
classic blue jeans
+
leather jacket
+
evening shoes
+
evening bag
=
<u>night out with friends</u>

Maxi skirt
+
white T-shirt
+
crew-neck sweater
+
trench coat
+
trainers
+
handbag
=
<u>day out shopping</u>

Let's try them again, adding some 20%ers:

OUTFIT WITH PERSONALITY

White shirt
+
straight-leg
jacquard-print trousers
+
blazer
+
ballet pumps
+
tote bag
=
<u>great work outfit</u>

Embellished velvet top
+
classic blue jeans
+
leather jacket
+
evening shoes
+
evening bag
=
<u>night out with friends</u>

Maxi skirt
+
white T-shirt
+
crew neck sweater
+
pink leather trench
+
trainers
+
handbag
=
<u>day out shopping</u>

If you love a minimal aesthetic but don't want to look dull,
you can include items with interest, such as an asymmetric
hemline or a textured knit, to help elevate the outfit:

ELEVATED OUTFIT

White shirt with asymmetrical button detailing	Long-sleeve body with cut-out neck	Leather maxi skirt
+	+	+
wide-leg trousers	classic blue jeans	white T-shirt
+	+	+
blazer	leather jacket	crew neck sweater
+	+	+
ballet pumps	evening shoes	trench coat
+	+	+
tote bag	evening bag	boots
=	=	+
<u>great work outfit</u>	<u>night out with friends</u>	handbag
		=
		<u>day out shopping</u>

These examples show just how easy it is to build a complete outfit from the basics that will work time and again. Then, if you swap in the pieces from your 20%ers, you have an outfit that is full of personality.

The outfits all have the same basic formula, but with few simple tweaks they suit any individual. This is how your wardrobe should be: formulaic, so every morning when you're getting dressed is easy but personalised so it's always with YOU, the individual, in mind. With a capsule wardrobe, you will always have the basics as the building blocks of your everyday outfits. But if you want to inject some personality, that's when style can become fun and exciting.

TAKEAWAYS

— The basics are the building blocks of your capsule wardrobe.

— They can be all different colours, not just neutrals.

— Make sure you audit them to find out what might need updating or repairing.

— Identify any missing basics you could add to your capsule wardrobe to help bring an outfit together.

— Starting with a base outfit using your basics, add some personality by swapping in some of your 20% pieces.

CHAPTER 5 WORKSHEET

How are you feeling about your wardrobe today?

Overwhelmed   On top of it

Your basics

Make a list of your basics; the simple pieces that go with everything. Don't include any trend items that don't form part of a capsule edit. I have added suggestions to the example on page 64, but of course the basics might be different for you.

Base outfits

Create three base outfits using only your list of basics.

1. _____

2. _____

3. _____

Now swap one item from your 20% pieces into each base outfit
to add personality.

1. _____

2. _____

3. _____

Are there any basics you might need to add to your shopping list?
Note them down here.

_____

_____

_____

_____

_____

_____

KEEPING YOUR

YOUR

06

CLOTHES FOREVER

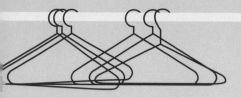

According to Greenpeace, clothing companies create more than 1 million garments every day. The Ellen MacArthur Foundation, a nonprofit that advocates a circular economy, highlights the fact that fast-fashion emissions will increase by 50% by 2030, if current growth continues. With such devastating statistics in mind, we can definitely take inspiration from the make-do-and-mend movement to prolong the life of our clothes.

Make-do-and-mend will not only save us money, but also provides a more sustainable way of living.

Over the years I have gathered lots of tips and tricks that can help prolong the life of clothes. There are some I adopt regularly and others I dip in to now and again, but all of them are great ways to keep clothes looking good for as long as possible.

Wash your clothes less often

Over-washing can damage clothes, resulting in shrinkage, colour fading and the breakdown of fibres. In addition, washing machines use a significant amount of energy, and break down microfibres and microplastics from synthetic clothing that ultimately end up in our oceans. As a general rule of thumb, here are some guidelines on how often to wash your clothing.

— **Shirts** 1–2 wears
— **Trousers** 2–3 wears
— **Day dresses** 2–3 wears
— **Jackets/blazers** 5–6 wears
— **Jeans** 4–5 wears
— **Wool sweaters** up to 6 wears (depending on if they're worn next to the skin)
— **Coats** once a season (including dry cleaning)
— **T-shirts and silk** usually after every wear (silk can be carefully handwashed using specialist silk detergent or dry cleaned)
— **Formal wear** 1–2 wears
— **Gymwear** 1 wear
— **Sleepwear** 2–3 wears

Deodorant and natural oil from your skin will cause some garments to deteriorate, so delicate items should be washed regularly to avoid spoiling. But many of us put everything in the wash after one wear, and this simply isn't needed. In fact, you can do more damage to garments like jackets and jeans by washing them than if you left them for a few more wears.

WASHING MACHINE TIPS

— Turn the temperature down to a cooler wash to help the environment and your heating bill.
— Don't over-stuff the machine.
— Turn jeans and jumpers inside out before washing to preserve the colour.
— Put delicates in a laundry bag to avoid snagging, pilling and stretching.
— Do up zips to protect the teeth, and other garments from snags.

If you have young kids or work somewhere where your clothing gets dirty, you will probably need to use the washing machine more regularly. There are always exceptions, but generally, if possible, it's better to wear an item a few times before putting it in the washing machine.

Spot cleaning

For those annoying marks you sometimes get on your clothing, spot cleaning is a much better option than a full wash. This is when you tackle a stain without washing the whole garment, using a damp sponge or cloth and some kind of cleaning product. My top tip is to have a selection of stain-removal products available so you can treat the stain straight away. It's always better to catch it before it dries, but if you do notice a stain that has already dried, try to spot clean it before washing it, as you'll have a better chance of removing it. If you love a home remedy, good old bicarbonate of soda is a whizz at lifting stains. Dry stains will benefit from a mixture of bicarb and water to form a paste, and you can treat wet stains by sprinkling bicarb on directly.

Hand washing

Even though it's a bit of a faff, hand washing is a much better and cheaper option than using the machine. This is because machines use friction to wash your clothes, which slowly breaks down the fibres in each garment. With hand washing, you have total control and can be more gentle in your approach. You can concentrate on areas that need more attention, like the armpits, collars, cuffs or any stains. It also uses much less water than a washing machine. Just remember to use cool water – it doesn't need to be hot.

Air drying

Using a tumble dryer for a single year emits more carbon than a tree can absorb in five decades, according to The Waterline. This statistic blows my mind, and emphasises the environmental impact of tumble dryers. Moreover, all tumble dryers release a huge amount of microfibres into the environment, which means it's crucial to stop using them or cut down on their usage. While it can take longer for clothes to dry in the winter, the upside is that it helps reduce carbon emissions and contributes to reducing household bills.

Hangers

Wire hangers are a no-no because they easily bend out of shape and can damage your clothing. They are also prone to rusting, which can transfer to your clothes. I've been known to keep a dry-cleaned jacket on the wire hanger provided, but I lived to regret it when one of the shoulder pads was damaged. Opt for slim, velvet-coated hangers that will save space as well as your garments. Your clothes won't slip off and the hangers will maintain the shape of your much-loved items. The other option is wooden hangers, which are probably the best choice for keeping your clothes looking good. But they take up a lot of room, so slimmer ones are always my go-to so I can fit more into my hanging space.

Garment bags

If you have large, expensive items, such as dresses or coats, consider storing them in garment bags, which will help protect them. Don't store them in plastic dry-cleaning bags because these can create moisture that can damage the fabrics. Instead, look for breathable bags that have a window so you can see what's inside. This means you won't have to unzip them all to find the dress you're after!

Moth deterrents

Moths are a nightmare. They do the most damage as larvae, so you want to attack the problem as soon as you spot any moths in your wardrobe. Prevention is always the best policy because by the time you spot them, it might already be too late. I like using cedarwood and lavender moth repellent, which can help, but if you are worried it's too late, you can put any items in a plastic bag and leave them in a freezer for a few days. This will kill the eggs and larvae before they get to work eating your beloved sweaters.

Armpit shields

These genius little shields prevent the harmful oils from your skin or deodorant transferring on to your silk tops and delicate T-shirts. You can buy reusable ones that can be removed and washed, or disposable ones that stick to the inside of your garment and can be discarded after use. These can help to prolong the life of the delicate pieces in your wardrobe that can't cope with the everyday sweat and oils they're exposed to.

Dust bags

Instead of chucking them away, keep and use the dust bags that your shoes and bags come in. The shops give you them for a reason: they help your shoes and bags last longer. They can help prevent colour transfer, sun exposure, excess moisture and dust. If you don't have any, you can buy them or make your own with some old fabric or clothing you no longer wear.

Alterations

Tailors are like magicians. If something no longer fits you, get to know your local tailor and see if it can be altered. Even if it's too tight, they can often find a way to let out a seam or take some fabric from elsewhere to make the garment fit again. You can have waistbands taken in, hems let down, straps shortened or even add a lining. If there's an item of clothing you really love but doesn't fit you perfectly or suit your frame, it's always worth a discussion with a tailor to see if there's a solution.

They can also help repair garments so you don't need to throw them out, such as a simply taking up a hem, re-sewing some stitches on a seam or fixing a zip.

TAKEAWAYS

— By trying to extend the lifespan of our clothes, you can save money and the environment.

— Wash your clothes less – it's better for them and more environmentally friendly.

— Avoid the tumble dryer and air-dry your clothes instead.

— Slim, velvet-coated hangers are better for your clothing and save space.

— Consider getting beloved garments altered or mended, instead of getting rid of them.

CHAPTER 6 WORKSHEET

How are you feeling about your wardrobe today?

Overwhelmed   **On top of it**

To help your clothes last longer, check you've got the following and use as needed:

☐ Moth repellent
☐ Spot-cleaning products
☐ Gentle-wash detergents
☐ Wash bags
☐ Armpit shields
☐ Small sewing kit
☐ Handwashing detergent
☐ Dust bags

Make a list of any garments you own that might benefit from being altered or adjusted by a tailor.

BALAN

07

PROPO

CE +

82 — 99

RTIONS

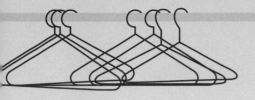

It's important to have a good understanding of your body shape and what you feel suits you. I firmly believe that we can wear whatever we want and disregard conventional advice about what suits different body shapes – but this is true only if we genuinely feel fabulous in our chosen outfits. If you find yourself not feeling quite right, it might be worth considering the benefits of the classic 'rules' about balance and proportion.

It's all about balance

The proportions of the body and the proportions of an outfit go side by side, but one is often disregarded in favour of the other. By understanding your body shape and the proportions of an outfit, you can get to grips with how to build the perfect look for you. You can easily learn your body shape and create an outfit based on that knowledge, but something might still seem a bit off. This is where understanding the proportions of an outfit comes into play, as combining both elements can lead to the best outcome.

Much has been written about the whole body-shape agenda and the 'rules' that are sometimes associated with it. I want to break it down and make it simple so it's not about boxing yourself into a particular shape – especially if it's named after a fruit – but giving you the information you need to make decisions based on your body proportions.

Accepting our bodies

All body shapes and sizes are beautiful and valid. Society and the fashion industry has led us to believe that certain shapes are more desirable than others, but it's all societal nonsense. We have all been fed unrealistic body and beauty standards since we were children. We've gone from the constricted, corseted bodies of the 18th and 19th centuries to the Kardashian shapewear of the 20th century. Although the diversity conversation of recent years has improved the situation somewhat, it's likely that the rise in body-related mental health issues in young people has risen, at least in part, owing to the idealisation of certain body types on social media.

The conversation around body inclusivity and seeing lots of different body types on our screens is so important. And not just seeing them, but normalising them. The average dress size is a UK 16 (US 12/EU 44), but this is just as it says: average. Some people are smaller and some are larger. There's no right or wrong.

These 'average' sizes can sometimes seem lost on fashion brands, especially high-end ones, some of which only go up to a UK size 12 (US 8/EU 40), or at best a 14 (US 10/EU 42). It's incredibly frustrating, and can play havoc with our self-esteem. However, it's not a reflection on anyone's worth. The female body goes through enormous changes throughout our lives. There's puberty, there may be childbirth, there's the menopause. All these life changes cause fluctuations in our bodies and we can change shape altogether within the space of a few months. You may have had a flat tummy all your life and now suddenly feel bloated and have gained 5kg. You may find that you had a slightly more rounded shape, but after becoming a mum, breastfeeding and running around after a child, you've dropped a few dress sizes. Bodies change, and it's important to realise that it's normal and okay. This is why it's imperative that we are familiar with our body proportions so we can get dressed confidently each day, knowing that our outfits work for the body we have. It's all about balance.

The proportions of the body

What we want to create is a balanced proportion, so that we have a good starting block from which to build our outfits.

Here are two illustrations of an outline of a body. The first one has lines showing how to determine your basic body proportions, and the second shows where to take measurements to determine your size.

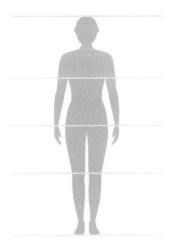
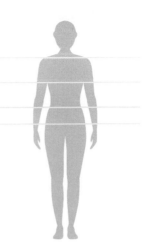

Proportional
Top two sections are almost equal to the bottom two.

Short torso/long legs
Top two sections are smaller than the bottom two.

Long torso/short legs
Top two sections are bigger than the bottom two.

Shoulders
Measure from the edge of one shoulder straight across to the other side.

Bust
Measure around the fullest part of your bust.

Waist
Bend sideways and measure where your waist naturally bends.

Hips
Measure around the fullest part of your bottom and hips.

If you have a small waist and wider hips, you can accentuate your shoulders to give balance to the hips (see above, left). If you have a big bust and a rounded tummy, then you can accentuate the bust and give structure to the waist with a rigid A-line skirt (see above, right). If you have wide shoulders and an athletic build, then you can give more shape to the waist and hips to balance out the shoulders.

The classic body shape 'rules' that we have all grown up with are made to be broken, and we can wear whatever the hell we like. However, balance is key, and keeping in mind your proportions and what works best for your shape will help when making shopping decisions.

Anna Berkeley, stylist and consultant and founder of Think Shape, a digital platform that helps women understand their body shape, shares this advice:

Balancing your own unique proportions is the single most important thing for dressing well. Consider how long your legs are in relation to the top half of your body – this dictates where your tops and jackets should sit, if you tuck things in or not and what types of shoes to wear with which pieces. Then, check your shoulders versus your hips. Are they bigger or smaller? If they are broader than the hip, then you need to either build out the hip – which can look fantastic – or shrink that shoulder. If the shoulder is narrower then you are best adding a padded shoulder or puff sleeve to balance it all out. It feels counterintuitive, but I promise you it looks good. Get these two things right and you are almost there!

It's vital to stay true to your style, rather than dressing solely for your body shape. For example, if you're considering wearing a ruffled top to achieve balance between your shoulders and hips, but you don't actually like ruffled tops, it becomes counterintuitive. Instead, focus on finding alternative ways to achieve balance that resonate with your personal style. For example, you could opt for big, bold earrings or casually drape a sweatshirt over your shoulders. Always prioritise your style identity while striving for proportionate dressing, otherwise you risk losing sight of what makes your style uniquely yours.

The proportions of an outfit

This is the fun part; when you can really start to understand why an outfit works and why it doesn't. Let's break it down.

If you want to achieve an outfit with an effortlessly chic and harmonious feel, paying attention to the proportions can really help. Striking the right balance in your outfit can elevate your overall look and create a sense of cohesiveness. By being aware of how different elements in your outfit complement one another, you can enhance the overall visual impact with a more put-together appearance.

Have you ever put on an outfit that technically should work, but you just don't feel like you? Have you tried to recreate an outfit that you've seen on social media, but it doesn't feel right? The balance isn't there. You need to balance out the proportions so the outfit doesn't look too one dimensional.

If you're doing the oversized trend, for example, you don't want to overdo it by wearing everything oversized. This can work for some, but for the most part, it's going to be overwhelming, and the outfit will swamp you.

Instead, stick to just one piece – perhaps an oversized blazer worn with a slim-leg trouser or pencil skirt. Or a pair of ultra-wide-leg trousers with a more fitted top. When it comes to shoes and accessories, look at the outfit as a whole and try to keep the balance going. For example, you could wear chunky loafers with slim-leg trousers and an oversized blazer, or almond-toe ankle boots or strappy heels with wide-leg trousers and a fitted top. Keep everything balanced so that the whole outfit looks cohesive.

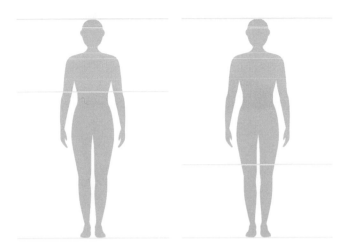

The rule of thirds

This is a great starting point when looking at the proportions of an outfit. Traditionally used in art, photography and architecture, the rule of thirds extends into fashion too. If you split your body in half with your clothing, it can look less flattering and more casual, and while there's nothing wrong with half and half, it's harder to get the balance right, and works only with certain garments. Instead, try creating a visual break in your outfit that divides your body in a one-third to two-thirds ratio. For example, your top might be one-third and your trousers two-thirds, such as a T-shirt tucked into a high-waisted trouser. This gives the look a cleaner, more put-together finish, helps to make your legs look longer and elevates your look. Give it a try.

Experimenting with different proportions can be an exciting and creative process, allowing you to discover what works best for your body and personal style. Whether you opt for symmetry or contrast, keeping the idea of proportion in mind will help you create endless effortless outfits. Remember, the key is to embrace the unique personal style that you set out in your Fashion Manifesto while being mindful of how each piece contributes to the overall composition of your outfit.

The unexpected items

Once you have the proportions nailed, you can move on to the unexpected items. We know why it's so important to create an edited wardrobe with an array of outfits that can be mixed and matched to look great every time, as well as how imperative it is that your wardrobe reflects who you are as a person. But if you are working, say, in a corporate environment with a hundred other people wearing suits, how can you still maintain that professional and smart look, but still have an element of difference?

It all lies in the unexpected item. This could be a bright shoe or a structured blazer, or a shirt with an unexpected collar. Or it can be in the texture of an item, perhaps a linen suit or a jacquard trouser. These are still smart and perfect for an office, but they give you an edge, a point of difference. This is when other people start to recognise and appreciate your style. Wearing a gorgeous tailored suit, white shirt and court shoes is fine, but swapping one of those pieces out for something unexpected? That's when you start to turn heads.

Remember when we talked about the 80/20 rule (see page 21)? The unexpected item can come from the 20% of your wardrobe, but it should also be something you keep in mind when buying a new investment piece. It's all about adding something to your outfit that makes it stand out. If you have a beautiful wool blazer in your 80% wardrobe, the unexpected part might be an interesting button detail or a high split at the back. Or it might be something in your 20% wardrobe, such as a bold satin top in the colour of the season, or a cut-out detail or an asymmetric hem – something that gives the item an edge. Or it could be a pop of colour in the form of a belt or a bag in an otherwise all-neutral outfit. It's unexpected and shows off some of your style personality.

Putting it into practice

Perhaps you're a new mum and have left a high-flying career for nappies and play groups. You love fashion and still want to feel like you, even though you're running around all day with a baby in tow. You may be wearing jeans and a T-shirt with trainers, which is a great combo, but it isn't very inspiring and you want a bit of your old self back. So maybe swap out the classic T-shirt for one with a drop shoulder in an interesting colour, or add a simple flat sandal with socks and an oversized chunky bracelet that doubles up as a toy for baby. Or, wear a cute, fitted linen vest with a loose-fitting cargo trouser and colourful trainers.

Adding those unexpected items that you love will show others who you are away from the corporate or the new-mum world. It will help give you a new-found sense of confidence.

Let's say you're in the market for a new blazer. Should you just click on the first link on social media that you like, or sit and think about what it is you want from that item? How is it going to fit into your existing wardrobe and work proportionally within it? Can you instead do some research and look at the different options that are around? Perhaps go and try some on rather than just buy online.

Can you find a blazer with an exaggerated shoulder or a structured, nipped-in hourglass shape? Or perhaps one with sleeves in a different fabric, or even a sleeveless one. And does it suit who YOU are, and most importantly make you feel good? It's sometimes those unexpected items that you get the most wear out of. These pieces are still classics and are items you'll keep for years, and they still fit into your capsule wardrobe. But they also have a different characteristic that will give you (the wearer) and others looking at you a sense of your personality.

If you go back to your style personality and Fashion Manifesto, as well as telling you what aesthetic you want to achieve, they give you points of difference you can inject to make a look your own. It's these unexpected items that change an outfit into a 'look'.

Time for an example

Let's say we have someone whose style is relaxed, and their Fashion Manifesto tells us they love modern, clean looks that are super comfortable, yet contemporary in feel. We can determine that this person loves fashion and wants to stay current, but also loves simplicity and timeless style. She will mainly want to wear flats or trainers and casual pieces like jeans, wide-leg trousers, T-shirts, knitwear and so on. The 'relaxed' style profile from the style questionnaire (see page 43) shows us this lady loves to wear items that make her feel comfortable. This could be a pair of khaki trousers, a soft cotton Breton T-shirt and some flat leather sandals. But her Fashion Manifesto tells us she's so much more than this. The clean element tells us she loves minimal and simple designs that are timeless. The contemporary elements tell us she loves fashion, keeps up to date with new designers and injects this into her day-to-day style. And this is where the unexpected item may come into play. She has seen a gorgeous fitted waistcoat, which on the website is styled with a matching blazer and drainpipe trousers. Totally not her vibe, but the waistcoat is calling to her and she really loves the style and fit. In order to create an outfit that's more 'her', she styles up the waistcoat with a pair of slouchy jeans, simple minimal flip flops and a soft leather tote bag. The waistcoat brings the modern element into play while the rest of the outfit is relaxed, comfortable and clean.

Let's take another example

We have a woman who loves a floaty dress, and whose style profile is bohemian. Her Fashion Manifesto tells us she's a bit of a maximalist with a spirited, artisanal edge, who also loves classic, peaceful pieces. From this we can gather that she is a creative who loves independent designers and has an edgy, fiery side! I see her in a beautiful floral maxi dress, suede boots and big jewellery. This is her happy place. However, she also loves a classic white linen two piece for the summer – not the maximalist look she normally goes for. It's unexpected, but still has the artisanal feel to it. She could style it up with beaded strappy flat sandals, a big, bold turquoise-blue necklace and a beautiful handmade basket bag, the kind you might find in a Moroccan souk.

Can you see how the unexpected items can create outfits that suit your personality perfectly? They help show the world who you are in a different way. It's important that you don't stay chained to your style norms – you can absolutely switch it up by adding different styles when you see fit. This is where Fashion Manifesto statements can really help, as those unexpected items are part of who you are and a style that is unique to you, not copied from someone on social media.

If you're a minimalist but want to add a bit of grunge into the mix, do it. Or if you love contemporary style but want to add in more of a classic look, fill your boots. Try on the item that's a bit unexpected, then look at how you can

95

make it work. If you love a relaxed suit but want to add a more structured tweed jacket, try it with a casual jean or loose linen trousers, keep the accessories minimal and the footwear more relaxed. Or if you are a bit of a rock chick at heart and love skinny jeans, slogan T-shirts and chunky boots, but want to wear a feminine, floral dress to an event, team it with some cowboy boots, a gold belt and some chunky jewellery. The options are endless. You could also opt for preloved or rental clothing (see chapter 14) if the item you want to try is a one-off that you won't wear a lot.

By adopting the practices in this book, you can begin to understand the nuances of style, and how it's so different for everyone. And that's a good thing! No one wants to look exactly the same as the next person. We don't have to pigeonhole ourselves into a style that we think is ours, either: we can be adaptive and fluid. Our style may change in different seasons, or one day we might just fancy a break from the norm. However, if we want to create a wardrobe full of pieces we'll wear time and again, our core pieces should encapsulate what our true style is. Then, when we build an outfit, keeping our Fashion Manifesto in mind, we can use those staple pieces and inject a bit of personality with the unexpected items we love.

TAKEAWAYS

— All body shapes and sizes are beautiful and valid.

— Work out the proportions of your body to see how different items will suit you.

— Try to create balanced proportions with your outfit.

— Stay true to your style, and don't wear something just because it suits your shape.

— Create a visual break in your outfit that consists of a one-third and two-thirds ratio.

— Add unexpected items that elevate your outfit.

— Keep your Fashion Manifesto in mind to ensure you stay true to your style personality.

CHAPTER 7 WORKSHEET

How are you feeling about your wardrobe today?

Overwhelmed   **On top of it**

Thinking about the proportions of your own shape, how could you balance out your body? For example, if you have bigger shoulders in proportion to your hips, you might choose an A-line skirt to balance them out.

_____

_____

_____

_____

Outfit proportions

Using your five key items that you pulled out at the beginning of the book (see page 19), how can you use other items to balance out the proportions?

Remember to not have everything the same. If you are going for an oversized jacket, balance it out with slim or straight-leg jeans, a high heel and an oversized bag, or a smaller bag and chunkier sandals. If you are wearing a slim-fitting suit with flat loafers for work, could you add some sculptural jewellery to balance it out? It's about creating an outfit that looks considered and interesting. You might roll up the sleeve of the blazer so it contrasts with the formality of the suit.

Note down some ideas about how you could make your five pieces more interesting and balanced.

Unexpected items

Using the ideas you've just noted, think about unexpected items you could add, such as a sculptural jacket or textured fabric, a bright green shoe or a fluffy bag. What could make each outfit full of personality?

Outfit 1   Unexpected item

_____   _____

Outfit 2   Unexpected item

_____   _____

Outfit 3   Unexpected item

_____   _____

Outfit 4   Unexpected item

_____   _____

Outfit 5   Unexpected item

_____   _____

List the unexpected items you already own in the space below.

_____

_____

_____

_____

WHY THINGS

08

DON'T FFEL GOOD

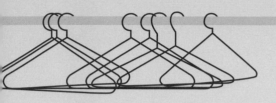

Have you ever put something on and it just doesn't feel right? Something seems a bit off-balance? Although you've been inspired by a street-style photo and meticulously replicated the whole look, it somehow doesn't hit the mark. Why is that? It all comes back to finding your why in your style. We are all different shapes, with different personalities and different lifestyles, so simply copying someone else's look or using a wardrobe formula is never going to suit everybody.

Subtle differences

Every body shape is different, and clothing is going to look different on different people. Traditional catwalk models are all straight up and down, very slender and tall for a reason – they have a natural simplicity that will not draw attention away from the clothes. When you have 20–30 models all walking the runway with the same body shape, the attention is taken away from the individual and becomes all about the clothes. Catwalks are all about selling the clothing, after all.

Add a shorter, more voluptuous model and suddenly the emphasis is on the body – not in a negative way, it's just that attention is taken off the clothes and the wearer's personality is shown more because the clothes fit in a different way. The line of a jacket will fall differently because it follows a curve; the hem of a skirt will sit lower on shorter legs.

The fashion industry needs to show more diversity in body shapes. And it's great to see more fun and personality in a catwalk show, as well as showing how different clothes will fit different bodies. These days we do see more plus-size and mid-size models on the catwalk than ever before, and I welcome the change.

In ordinary life too, a 1.75m (5ft 9in) curvy frame with a big bust wearing an oversized double-breasted suit is going to look very different from a 1.55m (5ft 1in) petite frame wearing the same suit. An oversized suit will swamp a petite frame, so she might prefer to wear the wider-leg trousers with a more fitted blazer. The size 16 (US 12/EU 44) person may prefer to wear a low V-neck fitted vest with the blazer undone so it flatters the bust a bit more. Every outfit needs adapting to suit the individual, so trying to duplicate a look can be fruitless and make you feel confused about your own style. But by looking at the outfit objectively and thinking about what feels out of place, you can begin to understand why an outfit that works on one person doesn't on the next. Remember the balance and proportions chapter (page 82)? When everything is balanced, an outfit can feel in alignment. If one part is out of proportion, then the balance is off and the whole outfit looks wrong. Keeping in mind the ways we can use clothing to balance our shape out will help us avoid making the wrong choices.

It's also important to stick to your Fashion Manifesto. If you veer off on a tangent because you like the look of something someone else is wearing, it can take your outfit way off course and result in a look that doesn't suit you and makes you feel uncomfortable. That's not to say that you can't recreate something you love on social media – you just need to look at it objectively and make it work for you, rather than attempt a carbon copy of it.

Let's take my Fashion Manifesto as an example.

I might start with a base – perhaps some loose trousers (relaxed). Now I add a fitted vest (effortless) and a blazer (elevated), some simple strappy sandals (minimal) and a textured clutch (contemporary). This works because I've ticked off most elements of my Fashion Manifesto. The only thing missing is the 1970s California element I sometimes add, but I don't need to include it in every outfit.

But what if I'd seen a floaty skirt I loved, and wanted to try it out? A classic way of styling it might look like this: the skirt (feminine) with a fitted vest (effortless), strappy heels (elegant) and a small clutch bag (elegant). While there's nothing wrong with this outfit, it's a bit too pretty for me: my style is more androgynous and a bit freer. The skirt, clutch and heels are too feminine, and even though each element could certainly work as a separate in my wardrobe, together they just don't feel like me. I know I would feel uncomfortable wearing this. Instead, I would pair the floaty skirt with chunky slides or trainers, or even keep the skirt and heels, but add a loose sweater to add the relaxed and contemporary elements from my manifesto.

If you ensure most of your manifesto is present and correct while building your outfit, you'll always be off to a good start. And you can always add an unexpected item, for example a bright orange earring or an amazing vintage bag. This is when an outfit will start to feel like you again.

TAKEAWAYS

— If something you're wearing doesn't feel right, first check whether it fits you properly.

— Check if the balance is right on your body. If not, how could you change it?

— Check if the balance of the outfit is right. Is it too oversized/too girlie/too relaxed? How can you add a different element in keeping with your Fashion Manifesto to make it look better?

— Check whether the outfit incorporates at least four of your Fashion Manifesto words.

CHAPTER 8 WORKSHEET

How are you feeling about your wardrobe today?

Overwhelmed   On top of it

| | | | | | | | | |

Think of an outfit you love that you've seen on someone, but that you don't think will suit you. Ask yourself what aspects of it wouldn't work on you. Think about your body shape, style, wardrobe, lifestyle and so on. Write down the reason(s) below.

_____

_____

_____

Starting with the outfit you saw as a base, create a similar one that incorporates at least four of the words from your Fashion Manifesto.

_____

_____

_____

Now create a second outfit by swapping out one item for another that incorporates a different word in your manifesto. Remember to include unexpected items that give your outfit individuality.

_____

_____

_____

THE M

108 ——— 115

OUTFIT

OOD

OF AN

9

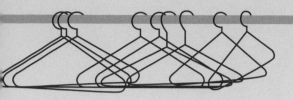

An outfit's mood is that mysterious appeal that you can't quite pinpoint when examining a look you love. It's elusive and enigmatic, but when put together it makes total sense. By creating outfits for different scenarios that fit the occasion and are well thought out, you've nailed the mystery and you'll be that person with the awesome wardrobe that always looks great in every setting or at every event.

Every time you head out, whether it's for a lunch with a girlfriend, a date night, a corporate work meeting or a play in the park with your kids, you want to create the right mood with your look. And with just one piece of clothing, you can create different outfits for countless scenarios. This is exactly how you want your capsule wardrobe to work, so that if you invest in an item, you know you'll get the wear out of it.

How to do it

Let's look at an example of how I would style a black ankle-length satin skirt in four different moods and scenarios, while keeping my Fashion Manifesto in mind.

1 — <u>Relaxed (lunch with friends)</u>
Satin skirt, racer-back vest, textured jumper over shoulders, bright red flat sandals and cross-body bag.

2 — <u>Playful luxury (date night)</u>
Satin skirt, triangle bra and slightly see-through, fitted long-sleeved top, oversized blazer, heels and a clutch bag.

3 — <u>Tailored and contemporary (corporate work meeting)</u>
Satin skirt, white shirt with interesting detailing, blazer, chunky square-toe loafers and tote bag.

4 — <u>Sporty and chill (park with the kids)</u>
Satin skirt, racer-back vest, loose striped shirt worn open, colourful socks, trainers and a big bag for essentials.

Using your own manifesto, think about how you would style a piece in your own wardrobe for these events and note down your ideas in the worksheet at the end of the chapter (see page 115). You can stick to the garment I used, or try a different one – it's up to you. Remember to add an unexpected item to your outfit, if that feels right. This might be a colourful shoe, a textured material or an interesting print. When you consider the different ways you'd like to wear an item in your wardrobe, you can see what might be missing and where you may find it useful to invest in something new, even if it's just a basic T-shirt.

When I look at my list of outfits, I can see that I love the idea of wearing bright red flat sandals. This would definitely be more of a 20% wardrobe piece, but I think I would wear them a lot. Let's see how I could wear them:

- In the summer, I could swap out the trainers I would wear to the park and instead wear the red sandals.
- If my workplace allowed sandals, I would happily wear a flat red sandal with an androgynous-style suit, maybe adding socks for a cool, unexpected look.
- I would wear them with wide-leg jeans and a T-shirt.
- I could pair them with a simple black T-shirt dress with a sweater over my shoulders.

This is how you can work out if a particular item would actually work in your existing wardrobe, or if it's just a one-time trend item that's not worth investing in.

Similarly, look at the basics that might be missing. In two of my outfits I include a racer-back vest, which tells me that this is something I wear a lot. Could I benefit from buying another one in a different colour, or maybe a cropped version, or one with a cutout detail? This would tick off the contemporary and elevated part of my Fashion Manifesto. However, I would need to keep in mind that, although I love a racer-back vest, I don't want to get into the habit of repeat buying, so I would invest in another only if I really believed I'd get the wear out of it.

The missing links

Make a list of any items you don't have that you feel would work with the pieces you already have in your wardrobe and help you get more wear out of them. These can be your 80%ers or your 20%ers. Would a light-coloured blazer fit into your summer wardrobe nicely? Would an oversized printed shirt help give your basics a touch of personality? Would an oversized clutch bag help bring your evening outfits to life?

Think about the mood you want to convey. Do you want to include a bit of humour in your outfit? If so, you could add an ironic printed T-shirt. Or perhaps you want to feel sleek, so you add some silk or satin and a delicate heel. Incorporating those elements, but keeping your manifesto in mind, will allow you to stay true to yourself, whatever mood you want to communicate.

Consider creating a Pinterest board and start saving outfits you like to the board. Look at what it is about those looks that resonates with you. Do these looks fit your Fashion Manifesto? How would those outfits work on your body frame? Do you have pieces in your wardrobe that you could use to recreate the outfits? If you haven't, and you feel you would get a lot of wear out of an item, then add it to your purchase list. Put your saves into different collections so that you can easily find them. Any influencer looks you love or any celeb style, save it all and you can refer back to it when you want inspiration.

TAKEAWAYS

— Think about the mood you want to convey every time you get dressed and look in your wardrobe at what item you could include to ensure your outfit delivers that mood.

— Each piece of clothing you own should work in multiple ways to give you lots of options to wear.

— Think about which items you could invest in that would help you wear existing pieces in more ways.

— Create a Pinterest board to save outfits you love.

CHAPTER 9 WORKSHEET

How are you feeling about your wardrobe today?

Overwhelmed   On top of it

| | | | | | | | | | |

How could you style one item in your wardrobe for different moods or events? Keep your Manifesto in mind and think about what you can swap in to make each outfit work to create moods to suit different occasions.

The item:

Relaxed and unexpected (lunch with friends)

_____

Playful luxury (date night)

_____

Tailored and contemporary (corporate work meeting)

_____

Sporty and chill (park with the kids)

_____

What basics might help you pull everything together?

_____

_____

Start making a Pinterest board or saved folders on Instagram of outfits and looks you love. If they don't fit in with your own style, think about how you could adapt them to make them more you.

THE GOOD,

116 ——————— 125

AND THE

10

THE BAD

UGLY

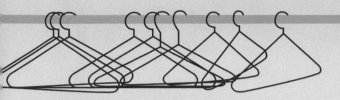

Many fashion editors have written about the 'rules' of dressing, from body shapes and what colours to wear (or not to wear) to what you should wear as you get older. I try to steer clear of rules as much as possible because fashion and style is all about the individual. If something makes you feel good and you love your outfit, that's good enough for me.

The good

That said, there are definitely some rules that can be helpful when building an outfit. In chapter 7 (page 82), we looked at how balancing out the proportions of the body can help you create a more streamlined look. Similarly, with an outfit, the proportions can feel off if they're not balanced, and I think about this when getting dressed every day.

Another rule we should abide by is wearing clothes that fit (unless of course you want to size up or down to achieve a different look). Size doesn't matter. It really doesn't. If something fits your waist and hips, but it's a size or two up from what you normally take, then that's fine. Unfortunately, sizing is never standard, so it's going to be different from one store to the next. Some brands have a generous fit, some are made for a boyish figure. It all depends on the fit model that each brand uses – but neither is right or wrong. The EU sizing system is based on measurements, which makes things easier, but each country is different, so double check first.

S/M/L	UK/AU/NZ	US	ITALY	FRANCE	GERMANY	JAPAN
S	6–8	2–4	38–40	34–36	32–34	7–9
M	10–12	6–8	42–44	38–40	36–38	11–13
L	14–16	10-12	46–48	42–44	40–42	15–17
XL/1X	18	14	50	46	44	19
1X/2X	20	16	52	48	46	21
2X	22	18	54	50	48	23
3X	24–26	20–22	56–58	52–54	50–52	25–27
4X	28	24	60	56	54	29

It's a good idea to keep a note of your measurements, including your waist, hips, inside leg, bust, shoulder and length (the distance from your shoulder to the floor). Some brands use measurements instead of sizes, which makes it much easier to buy the right size. Don't worry if the size is different to what you expected; what's important is how the garment looks on you.

The one other fashion rule I swear by is to dial it back when it comes to wearing multiple logos. If you're carrying a Gucci bag, don't wear a YSL belt. Or if you're styling up Nike trainers, avoid wearing an Adidas tracksuit with them. I think one logo on show is enough, and if you love the quiet luxury trend, then no logos is the hard-and-fast rule.

The bad and the ugly

For every rule we should follow, there are countless others we should ignore. Let's go over a few here.

Don't wear black and navy together

WRONG! Combining black and navy in an outfit can create a stunningly chic and sophisticated look. Picture this: a stylish ensemble featuring a pair of well-tailored, slim-fit black trousers paired with a slightly loose-fitting navy sweater, adorned with the perfect accessory: a pair of oversized black sunglasses that exude an air of timeless elegance. The combination of these classic and versatile colours results in a seamless and polished appearance ideal for several occasions, including a professional work setting.

To elevate the outfit further, add a pair of white loafers for a crisp, modern twist and provide a refreshing contrast to the dark hues. Alternatively, opt for a vibrant, colourful bag that complements the look, injecting a playful and edgy vibe. Embracing the magic of black and navy together not only creates a great work outfit, but also celebrates the art of mixing and matching, where the colours and textures harmoniously play off one another to create an outfit that truly reflects your unique style.

Stick to one print only

WRONG! Experimenting with mixing and matching prints can yield fabulous results. A clever approach is to embrace one dominant print alongside a more understated pattern, to ensure the prints harmonise rather than clash. For example, animal prints can serve as a versatile, more neutral pattern, particularly when opting for darker shades. Alternatively, you can explore a cohesive look by sticking to prints that share similar colours, such as pairing a striped shirt with patterned trousers. This creates a balanced look that effortlessly draws attention without overwhelming the eye.

Another option is to play with variations of the same print, introducing a variety of colours to add a point of difference to the outfit. This allows you to create a personalised style that showcases your creativity. By thoughtfully blending prints, you can craft visually stunning outfits that make a bold statement. Embrace the art of print mixing and you'll discover a whole new realm of fashion possibilities that capture attention and spark joy in your daily wardrobe choices.

Dress your age

WRONG! This is one of the rules that I find most detestable. Age is merely a number, and whether you're 25 or 65, your fashion choices should remain unrestricted. There is no arbitrary cut-off point dictating what you can or cannot wear based on your age. If your heart desires a bold cut-out dress that exudes confidence, or a stunning pair of snakeskin killer boots that unleash your inner goddess, then by all means, embrace it, regardless of your age!

The beauty of fashion lies in its capacity to empower individuals to express themselves authentically. It should never be a matter of conforming to societal norms or adhering to rigid guidelines based on age. Rather, fashion should serve as a medium through which you can celebrate your uniqueness and explore the myriad facets of your personal style. Embrace the freedom to make sartorial choices that resonate with your soul and make you feel beautiful and confident, irrespective of the number of years with which you've graced this world.

Match your shoes and handbag

WRONG! Matching accessories can create a sense of an outfit being too put-together. For a more interesting look, consider introducing a touch of juxtaposition. Rather than aiming for perfect matches, opt for coordinated items that complement the overall look without matching completely. You can achieve this by picking a colour from your dress or your jewellery that harmonises with the rest of the outfit.

Alternatively, incorporate unexpected pieces that allow your unique style personality to shine through. Embrace the beauty of contrasts and experiment with elements that add a twist to your outfit. This approach not only adds excitement and depth to your look, but also gives you the freedom to express yourself authentically.

Don't mix jewellery metals

WRONG! Stacking up necklaces in both gold and silver is a chic way to elevate your jewellery game. The combination of these two metals adds sophistication and modernity to any outfit. Similarly, don't hesitate to mix and match your metal bracelets and rings for a dynamic and eye-catching effect. This bold approach to accessorising allows you to showcase your style and love for experimentation. Don't shy away from the beauty of mixed metals, as it adds a gorgeous element of versatility and charm to your overall look.

Don't wear red and pink together

WRONG! The combination of red and pink can create a stunning and impactful look when the tones are coordinated well. To achieve a harmonious blend, opt for colour blocking rather than adding too many elements. This will ensure that the red and pink shades complement each other seamlessly, enhancing the overall visual appeal. Alternatively, you can highlight one colour as the hero hue and introduce the other as an accent through accessories. This approach is subtler, allowing you to showcase your style with finesse. Whether you choose to embrace bold colour blocking or add subtle accents, the pairing of red and pink promises a fashion-forward statement that exudes confidence and elegance.

Forget the rules

Fashion is a playground of creativity and self-expression, where rules are meant to be broken. It's all about embracing what makes you feel confident and genuinely happy with your outfit choices. When you dress in a way that reflects your inner desires and personality, there's a special glow that comes from within. It's empowering to curate a look that aligns perfectly with who you are, and it opens up a world of freedom to explore and experiment.

Fashion guidelines and styling tips can be helpful, like friendly nudges in the right direction. They can guide you on what might work well for your body shape, your colour preferences or the occasion. But remember, the final decision is in your hands! Trust your intuition and confidence to create outfits that feel like a true reflection of yourself.

So go ahead and be bold! Fearlessly mix patterns, combine colours that ignite your passion, and wear silhouettes that make you feel like a work of art. Fashion is a journey towards becoming your best and most authentic self, celebrating the magic of wearing your soul on the outside and radiating joy from within. Embrace the adventure and make fashion uniquely yours!

TAKEAWAYS

— Rules are made to be broken. You do you!

— If something makes you feel good, wear it.

— Don't worry about sizes. Wear what fits, the labels don't matter.

— Keep a note of your measurements.

— Be creative and bold. Fashion is meant for self-expression.

CHAPTER 10 WORKSHEET

How are you feeling about your wardrobe today?

Overwhelmed   On top of it

Note down your body measurements here.

Bust	Waist	Hips	Shoulders	Back	Length (shoulder to floor)	Inside leg

Good rules

Note down any rules or tips you've heard that you think may help you.

_____

_____

_____

Outdated rules

Note down any rules that you'd like to try breaking. Perhaps you want to experiment with wearing black and navy together, or mixing gold and silver?

_____

_____

_____

UR +

11

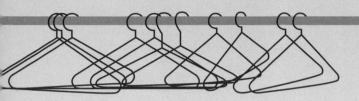

Although anything goes when it comes to the rules, when we're talking about colour and print, there are some colours that work better together than others. You don't want the garments you wear to be competing with each other. You want them to complement each other, so that you are wearing the clothes, rather than them wearing you!

Colour rules

Colour analysis (or having your colours 'done') is something I haven't really got on board with, because I like to break the rules. However, I do agree that some people might suit a warmer shade of white or a more orange-toned red, and that it can be beneficial for people to understand what suits them. It can help to get advice from a professional on what shades your skin tone suits – the key is not to feel tied down by the results. It's more of a helpful guide to assist you while shopping. If your colour chart suggests avoiding something you absolutely love, like a lemon-yellow sundress, don't feel obliged to follow it. You can still wear that fabulous dress, and simply opt for a colour that suits your skin tone better in other elements of your outfit.

There's always a way to work around it. For example, if you love olive tones but olive is not on your 'recommended' list, don't feel you can never wear that shade of green again. You could try wearing an olive-green trouser or skirt, instead of having the colour near your face. It's all about finding what makes you feel confident. The rigid approach that some colour therapists take can make it feel like you must fit into specific categories, and this doesn't sit well with me. It's just another rule that makes getting dressed difficult. We are all unique, and fashion should be about embracing our individuality, not conforming to strict rules. Let's celebrate the diversity of colours and styles and wear what makes us feel amazing, no matter what some chart says!

The colour wheel

The colour wheel is a great tool to help you work out what colours and tones complement each other, and this will help if you want to add some brights and mix-and-match colours together. I tend to wear a bit more colour in the warmer months as I like how it looks when I have a bit of a tan, and then I go back to darker hues in autumn. But you may be a colour lover all year round, or perhaps you like to brighten up those gloomy winter days with a pop of something bright.

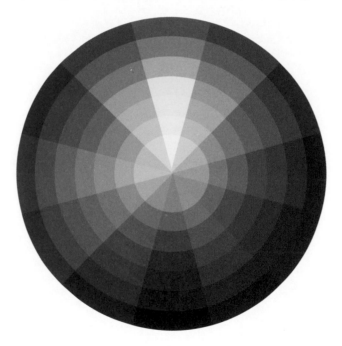

When approaching colour mixing, always think about pulling it back a bit. If you have more than three bright colours in an outfit, add texture or different fabrics and unexpected items to ensure your look remains modern and cool, rather than full-on children's entertainer.

If you struggle to move away from your all-black outfits but want to experiment a bit more, you can venture into colour going just one step in on the colour wheel. This will give a really chic look with a bit more depth. Remember to think about texture and those modern elements like sculptural pieces, cargo pockets or interesting details.

Alternatively, add a pop of colour with a bright accessory. When added to neutrals, this can make a simple outfit look interesting and modern – think bright earrings or shoes, or a bright bag. If you mix the neutrals so the colours are not all one-dimensional, your outfit becomes considered and cool.

Tones

Keeping tones similar head-to-toe will create a streamlined look, while still adding colour. If you go down the colour wheel into the centre, all those tones will work together to create a considered look.

Texture

If your outfit incorporates two distinct colours, introducing some texture can enhance its visual appeal. Consider incorporating elements like a fuzzy bag, a vinyl coat or textured shoes. These additions will give your outfit more depth and interest.

Colour blocking Rather than mixing colours randomly, stick to a colour-blocked look. Colours that work best for this are usually bright and can either lie on the opposite sides of the colour wheel or next to each other.

Analogous tones The colours next to each other on the colour wheel are called analogous tones. These will work well together because they can be less abrasive. For example, red and pink, blue and green, orange and yellow, and so on.

Complementary colours Opposite colours of the colour wheel are called complementary colours. You can then move down the wheel to mix different tones. This is a flattering way to wear colour because they complement one another.

Neutrals Experiment with neutrals. If you love black, bring in tones of brown, khaki, navy, grey and so on. If you love whites, bring in tones of cream, pale pastels, pale greys and so on. This will bring depth to your outfit so that it's not so one-dimensional.

Denim is considered a neutral, so it's a great place to start when introducing new colours. You can mix your hues of denim for a double-denim look, or add different colours as a starting point from which to experiment.

To wear colour well, you want to ensure the colours are not too busy: you want the eye to take in the outfit as a cohesive look that's not competing with itself. For example, you might pair a really bright red coat with a pair of grey trousers, a simple white shirt and an animal-print shoe. Nothing is competing with the coat, which is the star of the show. This is why I don't think red and black go particularly well together; black clashes with the red, there's no harmony there, and it's much better to use a lighter neutral that doesn't grate.

That's not to say you can't wear a whole outfit of colour, but if you do, keep the colours balanced, and remember to add texture and a bit of friction. Don't add lots of different colours from different parts of the colour wheel, as your outfit will feel chaotic with no cohesion. Instead, begin by experimenting with the analogous tones or complementary colours.

Mixing prints

Mixing prints can be so satisfying, and look beautiful. It doesn't have to be scary. A print mix can make a real statement, but it can also be subtle, using delicate prints and muted colours.

The key is to include something gritty into the mix, like texture or structure. When prints are mixed well, it's usually because something striking has been added, which allows the outfit to move and breathe. It could be something like shiny leather or see-through organza; it could be a stiff fabric like jacquard or taffeta; it could be a fluffy jumper or a fur coat. Using structure, it could be a nipped-in structured coat or a shoulder pad, an interesting architectural bag or organic asymmetric hemline. Remember when we talked about unexpected items (see page 92)? This is the same concept. Those interesting elements added to a print clash make for a really striking outfit that looks considered and powerful.

Another way to mix prints is to take two contrasting styles of print. For example, a pretty floral top with a more androgynous camouflage trouser, or a manly stripe shirt with a more feminine print on the bottom half. That juxtaposition of styles makes the look more interesting – it's always worth experimenting.

When it comes to mixing colour and print in your capsule wardrobe, think about what you already have in your wardrobe and work out how these items will fit within it. Can you create multiple outfits? Are you avoiding short-lived trends? Is it something you will have in your wardrobe for years?

If the answer is no to any of these, it might not be the right piece to invest in. That's not to say that print and colour isn't for you, it might be that you just haven't found the right garment yet. You want the item to fit in with your existing wardrobe, but also have enough interest to make it thought-provoking. Ask yourself the question: does this have enough texture or structure to make the cut?

If your wardrobe is mainly dark colours and neutrals, think about adding in a more muted colour that will blend more easily. Bright colours with neutrals can and do look incredible, but if you are not ready to embrace brights yet, do it in stages. Add a darker hue of red rather than a bold one, or a pastel print instead of a really busy bright one.

Similarly, if you love bright colours and prints but sometimes feel mixing them makes you look too over the top, think about adding a more neutral or dark colour that will act as a blending piece to allow the main colour to stand out. If you remember to focus on the hero piece of the outfit and not try to outdo it, you should be okay.

TAKEAWAYS

— Don't be ruled by the colours you think suit you; always remember your Fashion Manifesto.

— Look to the colour wheel for help on finding colours that work together.

— If pairing colour with black, look at whether it's a warm or a cool black and pair accordingly, but stay away from primary colours and black.

— To mix prints: keep one print bold and one print subtle, or use the same print in different colours.

— Add texture or structure when wearing colour and prints, to make the whole outfit more interesting.

CHAPTER 11 WORKSHEET

How are you feeling about your wardrobe today?

Overwhelmed   On top of it

| | | | | | | | | |

What colours would you like to experiment with, based on your own style?

Tonal
_____

Texture
_____

Colour-blocking
_____

Analogous
_____

Contrasting
_____

How can you mix prints according to your own style? Can you add texture, structure or different fabrics to add more dimensions to the outfit?

_____

_____

_____

_____

_____

Thinking about your own wardrobe, how could you mix more prints in with the items you already have?

_____

_____

_____

_____

_____

ACCESSORIES

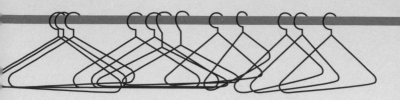

ACCESSORY (NOUN): A thing that can be added to something else in order to make it more useful, versatile or attractive.

Accessories can be anything, from shoes, bags and jewellery to socks, scarves and hairbands. They can play a vital role in transforming an outfit from basic to amazing in just one second, and can add a touch of personality without you having to spend a fortune or completely change your outfit.

Fashion editors the world over have always emphasised the importance of choosing the right accessories to enhance a look and how styling them in certain ways can elevate an outfit in a really simple yet effective way.

Adding accessories can help take your outfit up a notch, as long as you use them wisely – they can also detract from what you originally wanted to say about yourself. I'm going to take you through the art of accessories so that you don't get overwhelmed or overdo it. Sometimes stacks of statement jewellery can really work, but other times it can end up looking too busy and a bit of a mess. Accessories are the easiest way to add pieces with an unexpected element, which really help transform your outfit to something that screams confidence and style.

Keep in mind your Fashion Manifesto, as accessories can play an important part in finishing off the overall look. If one of your words is preppy, but you're wearing a simple, grey skirt suit for work, then you could add in a pair of round-frame glasses or some ankle socks with loafers. If you're a classic girl at heart, then you could add a beautiful silk scarf round your neck for that chic French girl look. Or if you love a relaxed streetwear vibe but also love 1990s style, you could wear the same silk scarf as a top with baggy cargo trousers to give a nod to that era while also making the most out of your accessories.

Accessories are
a reflection of you

The key to crafting truly remarkable style lies in knowing yourself inside out. Your accessories should be an authentic extension of your brilliant self; they should complement and enhance your style to make you feel confident and beautiful. Whether it's dainty jewellery that adds a touch of elegance or bold statement pieces, each accessory should reflect your individuality.

Not all accessories go with every outfit, so take a look at the outfit as a whole and think of the accessories as part of the completed look, rather than something you add just before you rush out of the door. Keep the following in mind:

— Strike a balance between simplicity and style.
— Choose accessories that enhance your outfit without overwhelming it.
— Accessories are the finishing touch that take your outfit from ordinary to extraordinary.

The transformative power
of accessorising

In the chapter on colour (page 126), we discussed how adding texture and structure can bring depth to create a captivating outfit, and accessories are an easy way to do this. You can transform a simple outfit with the addition of a tweed bag, a fluffy knitted scarf or a necklace with a big, tactile pendant. The contrast between textures creates interesting combinations that help you achieve a dynamic look, even if the individual pieces of your outfit are relatively simple.

A pop of colour

If you wear mainly neutrals, but would like to add a bit of colour, accessories are a great way to do this. I love to wear a pair of jeans and a simple black top with bright yellow or blue shoes, or a pop of colour with a bright clutch. These eye-catching accessories draw attention and create visual interest to make your outfit more exciting without compromising your style personality.

Texture and structure

Alternatively, wearing accessories that work in harmony with your outfit can create a streamlined, cohesive look – just remember to add an interesting texture or structure to ensure your look still has a sense of modernity. If you love minimal accessories that have clean lines and subtle detailing, a pair of simple hoop earrings, a thin belt or a delicate bangle can add a touch of refined elegance without compromising your style.

The balancing act

Accessories can also help create a sense of balance and proportion that complements and enhances the overall aesthetic. For example, a belt can help define the waist, a statement necklace can draw the eye up and give emphasis to the bust or accentuate the neckline, a pair of longer-length earrings can help elongate a rounded face, a pair of heels in your skin colour can help create the illusion of longer legs or a chunky shoe can add proportion. The scale and size of your accessories can also make your outfit really impactful. Sometimes the juxtaposition between an outfit style and the accessories help to make a boring outfit more playful and modern. For example, a fitted blazer and jeans paired with an oversized bright leather clutch, or a soft asymmetric satin dress teamed with chunky boots or sandals. If you consider how something looks together, and always try to add some modern elements, accessorising becomes a really important and necessary part of your styling routine.

Experimentation

Accessories give you the opportunity to experiment a bit with your style, too. Trends come and go, and accessories allow you to delve into that fashion space and be a bit more playful without investing heavily in a look that might last only one season. If you pay attention to the details, this is often where the magic happens, and it can be what makes all the difference. Thoughtful details like intricate beading, distinctive patterns and bold colours can all help to make a subtle but stylish impact. For example, a pair of colourful socks and sandals, a beautiful painted brooch or irregular-shaped earrings can instantly elevate your outfit, taking it to the next level in style. And it can also provide a lovely talking point over dinner!

Here are some ideas to help you:

— Add socks to shoes and sandals.
— Sunglasses are really important. They're a really great way to update your look.
— Stack rings and necklaces.
— Add a big belt around your coat or blazer.
— Hats are underrated. Add a bucket hat or a cap for cool-girl vibes.
— Think about the height of your boot. Don't allow any skin to show under skirts, unless it's a mini.
— Oversize your bag for instant coolness.
— Use haberdashery: colourful ribbon looks great tied round a low ponytail or plait.

Timeless accessories

It's important to focus on quality and invest in accessories that are well crafted and made from materials that will last, such as a beautiful investment watch or a belt made with gorgeous Italian leather. Your accessories can make or break an outfit, so you want to ensure that you finish it off with well-designed, thoughtful pieces.

Accessories are key to elevating any outfit from dull to amazing. They can add texture, colour and balance and help showcase your individual style to the world. If you carefully select your accessories and learn how styling them in different ways can transform your outfits, you will have extra tools to add to your fashion arsenal when getting ready each day. Don't be afraid to experiment, but always keep your Fashion Manifesto in mind so that your accessories enhance, but don't overpower your overall look.

TAKEAWAYS

— Accessories can transform and elevate an outfit.

— Accessories are a reflection of you.

— Be bold with your accessories – this is a great way to add your personality to an outfit.

— Accessories can help with balance and proportion.

— Don't be afraid to experiment with accessories.

— Look at your outfit as a whole, including your accessories to ensure it's cohesive.

— Invest in the best accessories you can afford.

CHAPTER 12 WORKSHEET

How are you feeling about your wardrobe today?

Overwhelmed   On top of it

List your accessories here.

Accessory	Is there anything that doesn't suit your style?	Do they work as an unexpected item?

Create two different outfits from your wardrobe. What accessories could you add to complement the look and add an interesting element?

1.
_____

2.
_____

Think about your body proportions. How could your accessories help define your shape?

SHOPPING ON 13

ON

13

A BUDGET

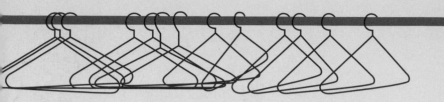

Shopping on a budget is a hot topic. There's a growing focus on sustainability and on fair treatment of workers in the fashion world. In 2023, one campaign organisation, FashionChecker.org, found that 93% of brands they surveyed weren't paying garment workers a living wage. Ethical shoppers want to support brands that care for the environment, reduce their carbon footprint and treat their employees fairly.

This is a step towards a kinder and more responsible approach to fashion, looking out for the planet and for the people who make our clothes.

But it almost inevitably involves spending more. Budgeting is tough, and paying for high-quality, ethical clothing can feel like a distant dream for some. Despite the desire to do the right thing, having limited resources can make it tricky to balance ethics with practicality. Fast fashion has conditioned us to expect low prices for our clothes, but sustainable practices and fair wages for workers make fast-fashion pricing impossible. The allure of social media and the constant flow of trends and consumerism fuels the desire to keep up with the latest trends. This has led to the huge rise in mass production of bad-quality garments that encourage a throwaway culture, which contributes to ever-mounting consumption. But the toll placed on our planet from the excessive waste generated by the fashion industry – predominantly fast fashion – is heavy. The devastating environmental impact calls for collective responsibility to curb the waste we generate.

Finding a middle ground means considering everyone's situation, from workers to consumers. We need inclusive solutions that respect diverse circumstances. By raising awareness and encouraging positive changes throughout the fashion industry, even starting ourselves at home with a commitment to buying fewer new items each year, we can make ethical shopping more accessible to everyone. It's about being mindful of affordability, exploring sustainable options and working together to create a fashion world that meets ethical values and budget realities.

To tackle this complex issue, we need a shift in consumer attitudes and industry practices. Encouraging consumers to invest in timeless, durable pieces and make mindful shopping choices may help reduce the demand for fast fashion and the resulting waste.

Moreover, fashion brands should take proactive measures by adopting eco-friendly and ethical production methods. Using sustainable materials, promoting recycling programs and ensuring fair wages for workers can all contribute to a more responsible and compassionate industry. Transparency in the supply chain will empower consumers to make informed decisions and hold brands accountable for their environmental and social impact. As individuals, we have the power to drive change by choosing not to support businesses that don't prioritise sustainability and ethical practices.

Connecting with our clothes

In our parents' and grandparents' time, there was a remarkable 'make-do-and-mend' mindset. Back then, clothing was built to endure, and the concept of fast fashion simply didn't exist. I was recently reminded of the wisdom in this approach during a conversation with my mum. As she reminisced about her early working days in the 1960s, she fondly recalled having two beautifully tailored suits. Those suits became her go-to outfits, artfully alternated until they genuinely needed a repair or no longer fitted. Back then, it was customary to treasure, re-wear and repair clothing until they couldn't be repaired any more – and we should aim to do the same.

How to find a tailor

Finding a skilled tailor has been an absolute game-changer for me. I've totally transformed items in my wardrobe, turning pieces that didn't quite fit right into ones that seem tailor-made for my body. I wear these items much more often now, getting the full wear out of them that I had hoped for when I first purchased them. It's amazing how a few adjustments can breathe new life into our clothes and make us fall in love with them all over again.

If you're unsure about local tailors, there's a wonderful company called The Seam that comes to the rescue. They link you with local specialist makers who can skilfully repair and transform your items. Once connected, you can conveniently drop off your pieces or send them by post for alterations or repairs. It's a fantastic service that takes the hassle out of finding the person with the right skills to rejuvenate your wardrobe.

An experiment

Let's try a little experiment, shall we? Think back to when you went through your wardrobe, deciding which pieces to keep and which to sell or donate. How many fast-fashion items ended up in the piles of clothes you're not keeping? Impulse buys may seem like a steal, but more often than not, those are the pieces we don't really need. They might be the clothes we were influenced to buy, but rarely wear. Or worse, they might have lost their shape after just one wash, or fallen apart after only a few wears.

It's easy to get swayed by the allure of low prices, thinking we're getting a bargain. However, we can end up with things that don't truly bring us joy and ultimately contribute to clothing waste. Next time you're tempted by a super-cheap find, pause and ask yourself if it's a truly worthwhile addition to your wardrobe or just another item destined for the 'not-keeping' pile.

If you take a moment to add up all the fast-fashion items you've purchased in the past year and calculate the total cost, you might be surprised. The same sum might have allowed you to buy two or three high-quality pieces that withstand the test of time and become wardrobe staples you'll cherish for much longer.

How to shop on a budget

When shopping on a budget, one piece of advice I endorse is to invest in the best quality you can afford, and focus on forever pieces that stand the test of time. Put simply, buy fewer items but of better quality. Of course, this is more feasible for some than others. However, regardless of our budget, steering clear of big fast-fashion giants and opting for ethically made, long-lasting garments – whether new or second hand – is a significant step towards a more sustainable wardrobe and making a positive impact on your purse.

Creating a capsule wardrobe helps us reconnect with where and how our clothes are made. By prioritising quality and longevity over quantity, we can avoid falling into the trap of wasting money on fast fashion. With this approach, regardless of our budget, we can make choices based on our personal style, what flatters us best, and things we know we'll love to wear repeatedly. It's a win-win situation that aligns our fashion choices with our values.

Shopping when you're on a limited budget can be frustrating, but here are a few tips that will help.

1. Follow the Forever Wardrobe approach by investing in a few essential items that will serve as the foundation of your capsule wardrobe.

2. Evaluate what you already have and try not to buy more of the same. Recognise the value of high-quality staples, like classic, black, wide-leg trousers, that already form the foundation of your wardrobe. There's no need to buy more of the same thing when you already have a pair that do the job perfectly.

3. Challenge yourself each week to style older pieces in your wardrobe in fresh and creative ways. Experiment with different combinations to create new outfits that will make you feel like you have a whole new collection.

4. Explore preloved, vintage or rental sites for affordable options. You'll be amazed at the treasure trove of nearly new or unworn items available at a fraction of the original price. We'll explore this more in the next chapter.

5. When it's time to let go of clothes, consider selling them. Even if you earn just a few pounds from each item, those pounds will add up to fund new items for your wardrobe that align with your personal style.

6. Consider hosting a swap party with friends, where each of you can bring clothes, shoes or accessories that you no longer wear or need. These offer a fun and social way to refresh your wardrobe without spending a penny, promote a sense of community and foster a sustainable and supportive fashion culture. Plus, it's a win-win situation – you get to revamp your wardrobe while decluttering your closet and passing on items for others to love.

7. For items that are worn out or need adjustments, find a skilled tailor who can mend or tailor them to fit you perfectly. By breathing new life into well-loved pieces, you can reduce your environmental impact and enjoy your most loved pieces for longer at a fraction of the cost of buying new.

Your shopping manifesto

These should be your cut-out-and keep key questions to ask yourself before buying something new. Why not take a photo of them to remind yourself on shopping trips?

1 —
Can this item be mixed and matched to create a variety of outfits?

2 —
Is it a fleeting trend or a timeless piece you'll love for years to come?

3 —
Does it truly embody your authentic personality and style?

TAKEAWAYS

— Invest in the best quality you can afford.

— Avoid the false economy of fast fashion.

— Consider timeless pieces that will last.

— Explore preloved or vintage clothes.

— Find a good tailor.

CHAPTER 13 WORKSHEET

How are you feeling about your wardrobe today?

Overwhelmed   On top of it

| | | | | | | | | |

How many fast-fashion items are in your donate/sell pile?

_____

_____

How much money could you have saved to buy better-quality pieces if you hadn't bought them?

_____

_____

What classics could you add that will help you get more wear out of your wardrobe?

_____

_____

_____

How could you style older items in your wardrobe in different ways?

_____

_____

_____

What items could you sell?

_____

_____

_____

PRELOVED

14

RENTAL

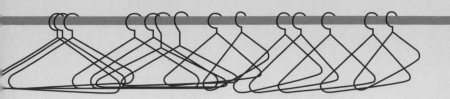

Shopping more sustainably and ethically is essential. Our planet is under immense pressure, and we have seen the harm fast fashion is doing to the environment. As consumers, we must do our best to counteract this. The statistics are shocking; here are just a couple:

— Of the 100 billion garments produced each year, 92 million tonnes end up in landfills. To put things in perspective, this means that the equivalent of a rubbish truck full of clothes ends up on landfill sites every second. (Earth.org, 2022)

— It takes almost 8,000 litres of water – the equivalent of the volume one person drinks in seven years – to make one pair of jeans. And when those jeans are discarded, they join the shocking amount of textiles that end up in landfills each year. (UN, 2019)

Melanie Rickey (@theenoughness on Twitter/X) is an journalist, writer and fashion editor who is an expert on living with exactly what we need, nothing more. She says:

> Once you see the impact fashion is doing to the world, you really can't unsee it. The clothing mountains in Kantamanto in Ghana and the Atacama desert in Chile are clear evidence of that. Clothes made from nylon and polyester don't break down, and pollute the planet for hundreds of years. It can all get really overwhelming, but there's a simple solution to this ... Buying only what you need, rather than clothes for a quick fix, is an exercise in patience and consideration. If you slow things down, you start to appreciate what you have and you can see what you need. Truly what more do you need than exactly enough?

Keeping it circular

As well as buying only what we need, as Melanie suggests, we should consider supporting the circular economy by buying preloved. I have bought preloved and vintage clothing since my teenage years; having access to amazing vintage markets like Portobello, Kensington and Camden in London made it easier to do so from an early age. There are now websites like eBay, Vinted, Depop and Vestiaire, as well as incredible independent vintage stores and charity shops both online and in bricks-and-mortar shops up and down the country. Many of these have a curated selection of pieces that are lovingly chosen, washed and repaired, so that you're buying a garment that's as good as new for a fraction of the original price. Even if you have historically been reluctant to buy second-hand, you can now buy with confidence.

I like buying preloved because it's not only circular, but also gives new life to something that was once loved and cherished. I often wonder about the history behind a vintage piece. Who was it worn by? What did they do? Is there a beautiful story behind the clothes? You're also less likely to be wearing the same item as someone else, and that's always a bonus. Remember that it's worth using a local tailor to adjust things to suit your shape, for preloved as much as new (see page 152).

Preloved sites are fantastic for finding great deals on clothing and an opportunity to make money by selling your own unwanted pieces. If you happen to own designer and high-end items, there's a plethora of resale sites available that will handle the selling process for you, typically taking around 40% commission. The beauty of this is that you don't have to deal with the hassle of packing and shipping; it's all taken care of by the platform. From start to finish, they handle customer service, making the selling process a breeze. My favourites include Curate & Rotate, The RealReal, Lampoo, Hardly Ever Worn It and Reluxe – and there are many more.

If you have high-street pieces to sell, platforms like Vinted, eBay and Depop are fantastic options. Remember, one person's trash is another person's treasure, so just because something doesn't suit you anymore doesn't mean it should end up in landfill. Embracing the second-hand market is becoming increasingly popular, particularly among the younger generation. According to research by Thredup in 2023, a staggering 83% of Gen Z individuals have shopped, or are open to shopping, for second-hand clothing. This growing enthusiasm for sustainable and eco-friendly fashion choices is encouraging, as it contributes to reducing fashion waste and embracing a more circular and responsible approach to fashion consumption. The global second-hand market is expected to nearly double by 2027, reaching $350 billion, so there is a really solid trajectory for growth for preloved items. Great news!

The beauty of renting

The rental market offers a fantastic solution if you need a one-off piece for special occasions such as weddings, Christmas parties, a prom or black-tie events. These moments call for something extra special, but buying a brand-new outfit might feel extravagant, especially if you won't have many opportunities to wear it again. Renting opens up a world of possibilities, allowing you to access high-end pieces that might otherwise be beyond your budget. You can find stunning options for under £100 to rent, and the services will also often offer accessories like jewellery, bags and shoes as well, so that you can complete your outfit in one place.

The rental industry's growth has been remarkable over the past decade. GlobalData predicts that the UK clothes rental market will be worth £2.9 billion by 2030. It's thought that 23% of the global fashion market could be made up from circular fashion brands estimated at $700 billion (Ellen MacArthur Foundation). This trend reflects a shift towards more sustainable and budget-friendly fashion choices, encouraging people to enjoy high-quality, stylish pieces without the commitment of ownership.

On the flip side, though, there has been much debate about the sustainability of the rental market and the true environmental cost of services like dry-cleaning and transportation. Some argue that rental might not be significantly more sustainable than buying new. However, finding a balance is key, especially for single-wear items needed for special occasions. In such cases, the rental option might well be the least damaging to the environment. It's essential to research and choose reputable rental platforms that prioritise eco-friendly practices. For example, platforms like ThredUp have a dedicated Fast Fashion Hotline and a sustainable model including sustainable packaging and full transparency. Hurr uses reusable packaging and green dry cleaning; By Rotation employs compostable post bags and partners with an eco-friendly cleaning and repair company; My Wardrobe HQ uses a green courier service and plants a tree for every rental made.

Ultimately, the key lies in curating a well-planned capsule wardrobe filled with pieces that stand the test of time and that you can wear on various occasions. Investing in high-quality, versatile items that you can style in multiple ways ensures you get the most out of your wardrobe. When you need something unique for a special event, opting for an occasional rental from a sustainable platform can be a fantastic alternative to purchasing a new outfit. It's all about finding that balance between thoughtful purchases and mindful rentals to create a wardrobe that elevates your style and supports the environment in the long run.

Combining preloved with your existing wardrobe

I love combining preloved treasures with new items, as the preloved piece often adds a touch of personality to my outfit, giving it a unique and sustainable flair. Instead of jumping on the latest trend bandwagon, I like to hunt for vintage or preloved gems that give me the same look in an eco-friendly way. And here's the best part: trends always come back around, so with a bit of searching you can often find something similar that's an original piece – much more satisfying than buying off the peg.

Let's take, for example, those boho-inspired floaty tops that scream Fleetwood Mac concert vibes every summer. You could splurge £400 on one from Isabel Marant or grab a high-street version for £20 from H&M. But the ultimate win would be snagging a stunning vintage piece from Depop for just a few quid. Not only does it look amazing, but you're also making a conscious choice that's kinder to the planet. Next time you're thinking of updating your wardrobe, remember that the preloved route adds charm, sustainability and a whole lot of savings to your style journey.

Take the blazer trend. It's been around for years, and is not going anywhere. If we cast our minds back to the 1990s, we can see images of supermodels and film stars rocking the blazer-and-jeans combo, and believe it or not here we are, 30 years later, still loving and embracing this effortless look. Here's a friendly tip – instead of splurging on a brand-new polyester blazer, why not go on a hunt for a preloved woollen one? Not only will you find a beautifully crafted piece, but it will be much kinder to your wallet and last longer. Plus, you'll be supporting sustainable fashion. Alternatively, if you like the androgynous look, another option is to go for a preloved men's suit and get it tailored to fit you like a dream.

When you're considering buying preloved items or renting an outfit, keeping your focus on your capsule wardrobe is super important – just as much as if you were buying something new. Take a moment to ask yourself: do you really need that floaty boho top? Will it effortlessly blend into your summer capsule and become a go-to piece you'll wear again and again? If not, then don't buy it. Let's be mindful of what truly resonates with our style and needs, and create a wardrobe that's not only full of carefully selected pieces, but is also eco-friendly. Embracing these diverse aspects of shopping will lead to a well-curated wardrobe, thoughtfully pieced together by you. By incorporating new, second-hand, vintage, swapped and rented items, you'll have a collection that reflects your personal style and values. It's the perfect blend of sustainability and self-expression, where you can explore your fashion creativity while being mindful of your environmental impact. Whether it's a cherished preloved gem or a trendy rental piece, each addition to your wardrobe will become a conscious choice that aligns with your unique style journey.

TAKEAWAYS

— Our planet cannot sustain the pressure the fashion industry
is putting on it.

— Buying preloved is a great way to keep fashion circular.

— Consider selling items you no longer wear to earn a bit
of extra cash.

— Renting can be a great option for one-off events like
parties and weddings.

— Mixing preloved with new can give your outfits personality
and a point of difference.

CHAPTER 14 WORKSHEET

How are you feeling about your wardrobe today?

Overwhelmed   On top of it

What preloved or vintage items do you own?

_____

_____

_____

Are there any wardrobe gaps you could fill by shopping for
preloved garments?

_____

_____

_____

Are there any upcoming events you could rent an outfit for?

_____

_____

_____

HOW TO SHOP WITH YOU

15

IN MIND

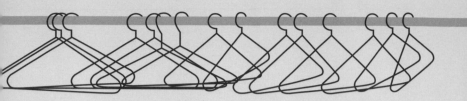

I'm all about staying true to
yourself and celebrating your
individuality, but it can be tough
sometimes. We're bombarded
with never-ending trends and it's
hard to resist the temptation to
hop on every bandwagon. Those
visually appealing images sneak
into our minds, whispering, 'You
absolutely need this!' repeatedly.
But staying authentic is worth the
effort, and we just need to take
a moment to remind ourselves to
embrace our unique style and not
be swayed by fleeting trends.

Digital scrapbook

My top tip for shopping authentically is to keep a digital scrapbook full of outfit images that you have gravitated towards. This could be an Instagram-saved folder or a Pinterest board, or just a collection on your phone.

When reviewing a collection of images, keep the following points in mind:

— Take your time to analyse each outfit.
— Do they match your personal style and manifesto?
— Do you have similar items already in your wardrobe?
— What items would you need to recreate these looks, and would those items be an asset in your wardrobe?

If you saved an outfit image that doesn't quite suit your style, think about what specifically attracted you to it.

— Is it the outfit or the person wearing it?
— Is it shot in a beautiful location?
— Does the outfit still appeal when you imagine removing it from the person or location?
— Identify which elements of the outfit you could adapt to fit your style.

Your wish list

By exploring and analysing your saved images, you can add things to your wish list that will infuse your outfits with personality, all while staying true to your unique style. Your wish list may consist of various items, so before embarking on a shopping spree take a moment to consider how each piece will integrate into your existing wardrobe. To build a sustainable and versatile capsule wardrobe, it's crucial to invest in pieces that bring you joy, you can wear repeatedly and offer numerous styling possibilities. Take a thorough look at your list and be honest with yourself.

— Can you envision at least three different ways to wear each item?
— Does these items align with your style personality and your Fashion Manifesto?
— Is this item a passing trend or something you'll want to wear beyond this season?

If you answer yes to all these questions, then it's time to make your purchase. You can be confident that the investment you're making will be truly worthwhile, as these pieces will enhance your wardrobe and align with your personal style.

Your wish list serves as your personal style compass, keeping you on track and steering you away from distractions. Think of it as your trusted ally, that helps organise you and saves you precious time and energy. With your list in hand, you can confidently navigate the stores, and avoid aimless browsing or mindlessly scrolling through online retailers. Each item on your list has been handpicked with care, and promises to elevate your wardrobe to new heights.

Think before you buy

Another good tip is to save items in online stores you like. Perhaps there's a beautiful two-piece that has caught your eye, but it exceeds your budget and you're uncertain about justifying the purchase. Or maybe you've been admiring a stunning evening dress, yet you're hesitant to invest in something you might not wear frequently. By saving these items in your shopping basket, you give yourself the opportunity to consider whether they are truly worth buying. You can choose to wait to see if they go on sale and, more importantly, you can take a few days to mull it over.

For many of us, shopping can become addictive and the act of clicking the 'buy' button can trigger a rush of the feel-good hormone dopamine, akin to a sugar rush. However, this fleeting thrill subsides quickly. By taking a pause and revisiting the saved item after a few days, more often than not you'll realise that it isn't something you must have after all. Did you know that up to one in three shoppers indulge in night-time online shopping, which has earned the nickname 'vampire shopping'? These nocturnal shoppers tend to spend about a third more than those who shop during the day. However, this late-night browsing often leads to impulsive purchases and subsequent regret.

If you fall into this category, fret not – you're not alone. Consider a simple strategy: when you catch yourself browsing late at night, resist the urge to click the buy button. Instead, save the item to your basket for a decision the following day or, even better, wait a few days. You may well find that your perspective has shifted, potentially saving you a significant amount of money in the long run. By allowing yourself time to reflect, you can make more deliberate and informed purchasing choices and avoid impulsive decisions.

As you begin to embrace your unique sense of style and gain a deeper understanding of your fashion preferences, your shopping approach will naturally become more mindful. Items that you once picked up without a second thought will now be subject to questioning, and you'll instinctively recognise whether they'll truly bring joy and value to your wardrobe. Once this realisation dawns, a sense of freedom washes over you and all those lingering style uncertainties of the past effortlessly fade away. You'll feel empowered to curate a wardrobe that authentically represents you, enhances your self-expression and increases your confidence in your fashion choices.

Shopping tips

These tips can really help overhaul your shopping routine. If you let authenticity and mindfulness be your guiding principles, the result will be a wardrobe that authentically embodies your unique style, values and individuality.

— Begin by meticulously curating a wish list of items that will complement and enhance your existing wardrobe and add value to your personal style.
— Do your research. Explore diverse brands and varied price ranges, and carefully examine fabric and fit. Ensure that the item you're about to invest in is nothing short of the perfect choice.
— Plan ahead. Think about where you want to go and plan dedicated time for each store. This strategic approach will keep you focused, warding off impulsive buying urges and ensuring that each purchase aligns with your genuine style needs.
— Prioritise quality over quantity: choose garments crafted with durability and longevity in mind. Invest in timeless pieces that can be expertly styled in multiple ways.
— Use the fitting rooms. When browsing through physical stores, take full advantage of the fitting rooms to ensure

the perfect size and fit. If you are online shopping, pay close attention to size charts and customer reviews, which empower you to make informed choices from the comfort of your home.
— Reflect before you buy. Adopt a mindful approach before hitting that 'buy' button.
— Be sustainable. Seek out eco-friendly fabrics, and brands that are passionately committed to fair-trade practices. Supporting these initiatives goes beyond mere shopping; it reflects your dedication to a more responsible and conscious approach to fashion and to having a positive impact on the world.

TAKEAWAYS

— Use a digital scrapbook to make a wish list.

— Interrogate everything on it to make sure it adds value.

— When shopping online, leave things in the shopping basket for a few hours or overnight, to allow yourself time to reflect before you buy.

— Plan your shopping trips carefully and keep your wish list with you.

CHAPTER 15 WORKSHEET

How are you feeling about your wardrobe today?

Overwhelmed On top of it

What's on your wish list?	Can you think of three ways to wear each item?	Do they fit your Fashion Manifesto?
_____	☐	☐
_____	☐	☐
_____	☐	☐
_____	☐	☐
_____	☐	☐

Before you buy something, answer the following questions:

Can I afford it?

_____

Why do I want it?

_____

Will it fit into my existing wardrobe?

_____

Does it align with my style?

_____

Am I buying impulsively?

_____

Is it a sale purchase I really want/would I buy it if it wasn't on sale?

_____

Have I given it enough thought?

_____

Will I wear it enough?

_____

Are there different ways to wear it?

_____

Does it have longevity?

_____

Do I already own something similar?

_____

Can I sell something to make room for it?

_____

16

TAKING A CLOSER LOOK

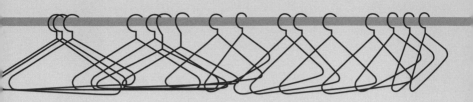

It can sometimes seem as though influencers are constantly showcasing endless fashion items. They proclaim that certain pieces are the 'must-haves of the season', and it can be exhausting and bewildering, even for those of us who work in the fashion industry. It's easy to get sidetracked from our true fashion goals and lose sight of what really matters. However, fear not! I have a few tricks up my sleeve to help you stay on track.

First, let's tackle the allure of sale items. Before adding something to your shopping basket, pause and consider whether you would have bought it at full price. If the answer is no, resist the temptation to make the purchase.

Another helpful tactic is to give yourself some time to think. Sleep on it, and you may find that the item you were contemplating no longer holds the same appeal or may even fade from your memory entirely. Next, consider how frequently you'll wear the item and whether it seamlessly fits in with your existing wardrobe. Can you envision multiple ways to style it?

Do you already own something similar? If the answer is yes, carefully evaluate whether you truly need the new item. If the new piece is an upgraded version of what you already own, consider selling the older item to make room (and a bit of cash) for the new addition.

These tricks will help you determine whether it is truly worth adding to your collection. It's important to remember that the more clothes we accumulate, the less value each individual item holds. If your wardrobe overflows with garments, each piece will not receive the love and wear it deserves, which diminishes its worth. On the other hand, if you curate a collection of thoughtful and cherished pieces, every penny spent becomes an investment.

I like to use the initials PTP as a reminder:

PAUSE　　Take a moment to pause and step away from the store or online shopping platform. Create a distraction for yourself, such as making a cup of tea or doing something else for a while. This break will give you perspective.

THINK　　Reflect on whether the item you're considering is truly needed and compatible with your existing wardrobe, body shape and lifestyle. Visualise how it would integrate into your outfits. Is it versatile? Will it seamlessly mix and match with other pieces you own? Will it complement your body shape and enhance your personal style?

PURPOSE　　Assess the longevity of the item. Is it something you can envision wearing repeatedly over time. Plan several outfits that you could create using the item, ensuring that it serves multiple purposes and can be styled in different ways for different occasions.

Reading the labels

To purchase the best quality I can afford has always been my guiding principle – but this doesn't necessarily mean the most expensive option. A high-end designer label doesn't automatically mean the fabric is any better than that of a more affordable high-street store. This is why having some knowledge about fabrics can help you make more informed decisions.

Regrettably, the quality of our clothing has been on a downward trend over the past few decades. With the emergence of fast fashion and the constant turnover of trends, brands are striving to meet high demand while keeping their costs low. This often results in the use of cheaper materials, leading to a poor standard of finishing.

The intended purpose of your clothing is just as important as the fabric's quality. While natural fibres, like cotton, wool and linen, are excellent for breathability, they may not always be the most sustainable option. Therefore, assessing the garment's intended function is key to making wise choices regarding its construction.

If you're looking at a summer dress, prioritise a breathable fabric to stay cool and comfortable. When seeking a winter coat, focus on a fabric that provides warmth and consider whether it needs to be waterproof or windproof. This will dictate the type of fabric to look for. Many high-priced designer brands use polyester, so always check the label, as you may be able to find a reasonably priced alternative with better fabric quality on the high street.

When shopping in store, take the time to touch and feel the fabric. High-quality fabric should drape gracefully and feel comfortable against the skin. Pay close attention to the seams, as they can reveal whether a garment is well crafted. Look for any signs of puckering and poorly finished edges. Is the stitching precise and straight? Are buttonholes neatly done, and are the buttons securely attached? Are there any loose threads or issues with zips and buttons?

The cut of a garment is the most telling indicator of its quality. A piece that fits perfectly can make you feel a million dollars. With age, I've come to appreciate that beautifully crafted clothing, thoughtfully cut and constructed, will always look better on the body. When trying on an item, assess how it flows and drapes. Does it accentuate the right areas and skim your curves gracefully? Or does it cling in all the wrong places and make your skin feel uncomfortable?

This is all part of creating a considered capsule wardrobe that works for you. Taking the time to really look at potential purchases helps you realign with your purpose, and will often stop you buying into trends and fads that don't conform with your new-found wardrobe confidence. It's a great way to get you to step away from the purchase and reassess.

What to look for

— Look at how an item is cut. For example, if a satin dress is cut on the bias it will skim your curves (this is the technique of cutting along the diagonal grain of the fabric rather than the straight line of the weave, to create a natural stretch and fluidity).
— Wear breathable fabrics that your skin will thank you for.
— Look at the label to see how the item is to be washed.
— Check the label for composition. Even though it looks like cashmere, it may be a cashmere mix. Check the percentage.
— Use your hands. Check whether a T-shirt is see-through, or whether an item bounces back after being stretched. Your hands are a great tool.
— Give it a tug. Test seams by giving them a little tug to see how well they are stitched.
— Think about what you'll be using the item for. For example, silk is beautiful but can be hard to take care of. Be mindful of how hard you want your garments to work, and for what purpose.

How you should feel about your new clothes

When you do make a purchase, it should bring you joy. You deserve a wardrobe filled with pieces that make you feel good, so occasional purchases within your budget are absolutely fine. Let go of any guilt or regrets if you've truly considered your purchase for the long term, not just a fleeting moment.

If you've bought online, once your item arrives, if you're uncertain about the fit, or if it doesn't make you feel amazing, don't hesitate to return it. Avoid holding on to something in the hope that it will eventually work out. Keep only the items that are truly perfect for you. By being selective, you'll avoid falling into the cycle of replacing the items you just got rid of, and find yourself back at square one. Choose wisely to create a wardrobe that truly reflects your style and makes you feel confident.

TAKEAWAYS

— Before you buy, remember Pause, Think, Purpose!

— When shopping in store, use your eyes and hands to check the quality of construction, the feel of the fabrics and finishes. If shopping online, check the fabric composition.

— Consider whether the fabric and construction is suitable for what you want the garment to do.

— Anything you buy should bring you joy. If it doesn't, return it!

CHAPTER 16 WORKSHEET

How are you feeling about your wardrobe today?

Overwhelmed   On top of it

Examine the label

Check some of the most-worn items in your wardrobe. Look at the
label and the fabric. Is it cotton, linen, polyester, wool, rayon, acrylic or
something else? Feel the different fabrics and notice the quality. Write
them down and, if you have time, do some research about the pros and
cons of each one.

_____

_____

_____

_____

_____

_____

When buying new clothes, look at the brands' ethos around quality
and environmental impact. Do they use recycled fabrics, or sustainable
synthetics like Econyl (made from recycled and waste nylon) or rPet
(recycled polyester made from plastic bottles)?

Remember, not all high-priced items are made from good-quality fabrics.
But all fast-fashion cheap clothing is made from low-quality materials. It's
always best to look at the labels first and then to invest in better materials.

AND ...

ACTIO

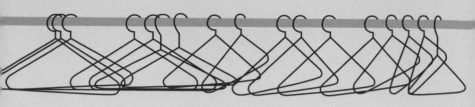

Now is the perfect time to put into practice the valuable tools you've acquired throughout this book. It's important to approach this process with compassion and understanding, taking a deep dive into your wardrobe and evaluating what truly benefits you and what doesn't. By learning from past purchasing mishaps, you can prevent your wardrobe from becoming a collection of items that neither suits you nor reflects your true self.

If you think it would help to better understand the reasons why some of your wardrobe choices haven't worked, try to take meaningful steps in that direction as we've looked at in previous chapters. Recognising and addressing any unhealthy patterns of spending on clothes could be an important aspect to consider. Seeking guidance from a professional who specialises in overcoming emotional spending habits might provide you with the necessary support to break this cycle. I sincerely hope that this book will help you achieve a harmonious and tailored wardrobe that aligns with your lifestyle.

By now you know your style and how it fits with your lifestyle; you've gone through your wardrobe to pull out the pieces that truly chime with who you are and how you want to be perceived; and you have a pile of clothes to donate, sell or store for six months. We've looked at the basics you need as the building blocks of your wardrobe, and how to use the 80/20 rule to help to bring your personality into your wardrobe. We've also delved into the proportions of the body and the proportions of an outfit to ensure you're wearing what is right for you, and we've shone a light on common mistakes and styling dilemmas that will help you understand what looks and feels good, and why.

We've looked at accessories and unexpected items, how to work out what is missing and how to shop with you in mind, along with incorporating preloved and rental pieces into your wardrobe to be more mindful and sustainable in your approach to shopping.

I want you to be able to put something on from your wardrobe and to understand why it works, or doesn't work; to be able to stand in front of the mirror and think about how you feel. And, most importantly, I want you to feel great!

It's now down to you to create your perfectly considered and stylish Forever Wardrobe that matches your personality and flair, gives you multiple outfit options and will serve you over and over again, so that you never have a bad outfit day. From now on, getting dressed will be easy, stress free and enjoyable. Don't be surprised when the compliments come flooding in – this is your time to shine.

Go for it!